SOLIDITY FOR DEGENS

An Uncensored Programming Guide for Blockchain Badassery

C.J FREEMAN

V.1.2

Copyright © C.J Freeman 2023

Published by Aquila Press Ltd

All rights reserved.

ISBN: 9798858885047 (paperback)
ASIN: B0CGKDJB5G (eBook)

'Whereas most technologies tend to automate workers on the periphery doing menial tasks, blockchains automate away the centre.

Instead of putting the taxi driver out of a job, blockchain puts Uber out of a job and lets the taxi drivers work with the customer directly.'

— **Vitalik Buterin**

CONTENTS

START HERE
Welcome to Solidity for Degens 8
What is the EVM? And What on Earth are Smart Contracts? 16
Making Your First Complex Contract in Five Minutes 20
Constructors: Contractual Foreplay 26
Basics made easy: Syntax, Comments, and Operators. 31
A Quick Word for Web 2 Devs 37

BADASS BUILDING BLOCKS
Variables, Visibility, and Basic Data Types 42
Data Types Two: Type Harder 49
Data Types Three: Type Hardest 54
Some Things Never Change: Constants & Immutables 64

Understanding Scope: Setting Variable Boundaries   70
Prefixes: Code Nicknames   73
Storage & Memory: Big Brain Not Needed   76

FUNCTIONS: THEY RUN SHIT
Making things Happen: Functions   80
Getting Answers: Return Variables   88
On Dial: Calling Functions and Handling Missed Calls   96
Snap Necks, Cash Checks: Payable, Solidity's Coolest Keyword   101

ALL GAS NO BRAKES: CONTROL STRUCTURES
If, Else, and the Art of Decision Making   108
Loops: Why Do Something Once, When You Can Do It a Trillion Times   111
Escape Artistry: Break & Continue   115
Events: The EVM's Facebook Posts   118

ERRORS: MISTAKES WERE MADE
Encountering Wild Errors   123
Putting Out Fires: Error Handling & Damage Control   129
The Perfect Contract Blueprint   136

Inheritance: Virtual Daddy Issues
                              139
Libraries: Borrow Brilliance   142
The End of The Basics: Preparing for
Intermediate Solidity   152

About the Author   159
COPYRIGHT   160

BASIC SOLIDITY FOR DEGENS

'Never in the history of agreements have you had contracts where the bigger participant couldn't get out of it, modify it or go to the person running the contract and tell them not to pay you. This will change the way that people interact with each other - it's like playing a rigged Carnival game versus a fair Carnival game. Why would I ever not play the one that's definitely going to work correctly?'

— **Sergey Nazarov**

START HERE

Welcome to Solidity for Degens

So, you've decided to learn Solidity?

Fucking. Sweet.

Decentralised systems are the future, learning how to power these systems (and create your own) with the ability to read and code smart contracts is a *very* smart move.

I am an avid decentralisationalist, and if you haven't heard that term before, it's because I made that word up.

I did so because there *should be* a word that describes someone who is for decentralisation to the degree that I am.

I began using Ethereum in 2016, and I stared writing my first Solidity contracts in 2017. Today, such contracts still fill me with awe.

So, this book is not only for new programmers to gain an understanding of the basics of Solidity, it is also (hopefully) an olive branch that will onboard a new cohort of developers into the world of web3. Notice I didn't say generation, as I believe anyone, of any age can learn these skills.

This book will also help anyone who works within a web3 environment that needs a basic understanding of Solidity code.

That said, this book will still help you if you are moving from traditional web2 programming into web3, and want to know how Solidity ticks at a basic level as a language.

And if you are already a programmer, the concepts we cover like *functions, loops,* and others will be very familiar, which is handy. The explanations I provide throughout cover these concepts as a whole and not just the Solidity syntax, so you will likely speed through them if you know the concepts already.

So, Let's Begin

I have another book, it's not a programming book like this, but it talks around why it's important to learn skills such as interacting with smart contracts.

It's a book on how to position yourself during the information age transition you are currently sitting through.

Yes, you, sitting there on your pert little bottom, are hurtling through a deeply transitional period in human history. This period will see the traditional nation state as we know it changed, drastically.

A basic run down of *that* book is, during this period, sovereign individuals with the power to bank themselves on the blockchain will rise. (The book is called *'Easy Money'*, yeah, maybe I could have named it better).

It deals with how you can better position yourself during the information revolution - but as you have decided to learn solidity, you are pretty much already there.

Like Ottoman's Turnip, or Liam Neeson in *Taken* - *'you are learning a particular set of skills'*, except instead of making you a nightmare for kidnappers, these skills are going to make you tremendously valuable, globally, during the next few decades.

This is because, as decentralisation grows, so does the overwhelming prevalence of blockchain technology. The future is coming. Fast. And the world is going to need a hell of a lot of passionate developers, soon, to build it. Yet, I hear a nagging voice from some of you...

'Whatever dude, I'm just in it for the money'.

Oh, good, so am I.

Aren't we all, a little bit? As the gold rush of web3 continues, developers of smart contracts are currently, and will continue to be, paid handsomely for their skills.

If I may again borrow from my other book, the changing way that humans work in the blockchain age will give rise to far more 'contract' work, rather than what we've known through the industrial period as 'careers for life'. This is good for you if you don't want to work for *'the man'*, and want to branch out to interesting projects, or even build your own DeFi protocol.

Right now, this contract work is being paid ludicrous amounts, and depending on how bad inflation has gotten at the time of reading, the numbers may or may not sound impressive to you; but it is not unheard of to have 2-3 weeks work paying upwards of $25,000. In some cases, with web3 security (my book on this particular subject may be out already while you read this, but finish the basics first) the pay can be $40,000 plus for security audits.

However. This is a book for *degens,* at its core. So maybe you've just heard about the ludicrous amounts of money people are making in Web3 by deploying ERC-20 clones called *'BigDickButtSonicCoin',* and tweeting:

'Alpha dropping! New (fire emoji) token, liquidity locked, devs doxxed, LFG big dick butt bros!!1! $BigDickButtSonicCoin

#bigbuttsonicarmy #crypto #memecoin'

Of course, this could be a real tweet, it's actually based off ones I've seen during the three bull markets I've been a part of. And who knows? *$BigDickButtSonicCoin* might reach a couple hundred million in market cap.

It's a crazy space to play in - and if you have the tools to navigate the tech behind it you will find yourself sitting in the 0.0001%.

Either way, welcome. So, onto more pressing questions – namely:

What the F*ck is Solidity?

You may have gathered, by my expert and completely unbiased calculations, working with Solidity is the best thing any budding programmer could do within the next ten years. By far.

So, *"what the Fuck **is** Solidity?"* you ask.

Solidity is a statically-typed programming language.

It was designed for implementing what are known as *'smart contracts'* on the Ethereum blockchain. At its core, it's a love child of JavaScript and C++ - raised by a pack of rabid blockchain enthusiasts.

If you've never touched a programming language in your life, I hear you.

*"I don't have a f*cking clue what 'statically typed' means, bro"*

Well, some other statically typed programming languages include C, C++, Java, Rust, Go, and Swift. If you haven't heard of these either, don't worry.

JavaScript, (if you've heard of that) is *not statically typed*, and is actually completely different from 'Java' as a programming language. Forget Java, it's for losers.

If you know any JavaScript, oh boy, you're going to take to Solidity like a fish to water. They are very similar, this book is not going to cover much JavaScript though, there are plenty of books out there for that - this book is almost 100% pure solidity.

As an example, JavaScript is *not statically typed* because you don't need to declare the type of your variables. A variable looks like this:

```
FavSexPosition = 69;
```

Here, you have declared that you want your program to save a number (69) to what's known as a *variable* (in this case, 'FavSexPosition'). The *compiler* (The thing that takes in all your code and spits out computer readable gibberish) just *knows* the data type - which is a number.

That's it, that's all you need to type in JavaScript to let your program know you're a freak in the bedroom.

However, in a statically typed language, like Solidity, you might declare a variable like this:

```
uint256 FavSexPosition = 69;
```

There's now a 'uint256' before the variable, to let the compiler know your fav sex position is a *number,* and not a *word*. (Technically, it's an 'unsigned integer' but we will get into the difference later. No need now).

This is because JavaScript is more of a 'high level' programming language than Solidity is.

Now, if you've ever played something like World of Warcraft (what am I saying, of course you have - you're reading a programming book, nerd) then you may think that approaching a 'high level' subject means it is harder.

In programming this is not the case.

High level programming languages are far easier to code than low level ones, you have to do far more work to code the lowest level languages as they are much closer to the binary machine code that is unreadable to most humans.

Solidity is only slightly lower level than JavaScript, and is definitely approachable for a newcomer.

Don't worry if you don't understand any of this properly, we have a lot to get through, and you may not have noticed it, but you just had your first win! All fucking ready.

You know the difference between statically typed and non-statically typed languages, you've just watched someone declare a variable in both forms, too.

You'll be coding the new Uniswap in no time.

So, right now, you may feel like a dribbling idiot every time you have to do anything more than simply open google chrome, but no matter, this book will take you from retard zone to wearing big boy pants, *reeal* quick.

What is the EVM? And What on Earth are Smart Contracts?

Just now, I mentioned 'smart contracts'.

As you are learning solidity, you may already have an idea of what a smart contract is. Yet, some of you will not, so I will to explain it regardless.

Imagine a vending machine. You put in a coin, press a button, and get a snack. Truly amazing, I know.

But in a way it is, because there's no need for a slow old lady, wearing thick coke bottle glasses, to check if you paid the right amount before begrudgingly handing over your snack. Human interaction? What is this, the fucking twenties?

Well, that's pretty much a smart contract - *a self-executing contract with the terms of the agreement directly written into code.*

There is no middle man, no *olde shopekeep* to act as an intermediary between you and your goods.

Of course, there are differences, the vending machine can only perform the most basic of actions, it isn't a full decentralised computer that can do what Solidity can - but the main difference we need to worry about is that of *trust*.

A vending machine is an example of a physical, centralized entity, whereas the EVM operates on a decentralised network of nodes, with *no single owner or central authority.* With the vending machine, trust is placed with a single entity, whereas in the EVM trust is established through cryptographic principles and consensus mechanisms.

Basically, the EVM cannot change the terms of your agreement, they are law. If the code was governed by a central party, it could take all your funds, or decide to charge you $10 for a coke instead of $1.

Solidity then, is the key to the castle in being able to let you write these smart contracts, which are soon going to be everywhere, from real estate and central banking to your hurried vending machine breakfast.

These smart contracts are stored on blockchains. There are many now, but throughout this book I'm going to assume that we're working with Ethereum, the largest. Ethereum competitors have even become Ethereum compatible these days - so even developers working on other chains are essentially still working on Ethereum.

Each contract on this blockchain is like a little autonomous agent living on the EVM (the Ethereum virtual machine). These contracts have a balance, can transfer Ether (the currency of Ethereum), and can interact with other contracts. They're like little robots that will do exactly what you program them to do.

What you *program them to do*, no more, no less.

But here's the kicker: once a contract is deployed, it cannot be changed.

It's like carving into stone. Fuck up the code? Too bad *hombre*, it's there forever. This is why learning Solidity has a massive focus on security auditing before deployment.

With Solidity, you can't patch a bug fix a week later, (unless you use what is known as a 'proxy' contract, but the point still stands, code is immutable once deployed). Yet, despite its quirks, Solidity is backbone of the *god-damn* decentralized finance (DeFi) revolution.

It's the language of choice for creating decentralized applications (dApps) on the Ethereum network. From token sales to decentralized exchanges to lending platforms, Solidity is the language that makes it all possible.

Solidity is a whole new paradigm, a different way of thinking about programming. It's currently the best way to connect the world for a better future, and learning Solidity can open up a world of opportunities.

So, are you ready to dive in? Are you ready to wrestle with the beast that is Solidity? If you're still reading, I'm guessing the answer is yes, then buckle up, grab a drink. and let's get started.

Welcome to Solidity, degens.

*"Code talks.
Talk walks."*

- Andreas Antonopoulos

__Making Your First Complex Contract in Five Minutes__

Alright, let's have a look at what a smart contract looks like in full.

In any other programming language, you would first learn how to get the program to spit out *'hello world'*, onto the console. We can also do this in solidity, it's pretty much useless, like all of these beginner exercises, but it will show you some key concepts.

In most programming languages, a "Hello, World!" program is a simple one-liner.

But this is Solidity, baby - A "Hello, World!" program in Solidity is a *deployed smart contract* that stores a message of your choice, and has something called a *function* to retrieve that greeting.

This program is a parrot. A shit parrot that only knows one phrase - but the cool thing is once you've deployed it, that parrot squawks forever.

My *'Hello World'*, program, therefore, is a *'Fuck You, Alice'*, program.

I can retrieve this message to my ex-girlfriend whenever I want, it's cathartic. In 50 years, I won't have to try to pull out a 50-year-old hard drive to try and run this program on windows 42, it will still be there, forever. *Double Fuck you*, Alice.

For now, I'll just give you the run through. You don't have to pull out some kind of code editor. Nor for this entire book if you don't want to. This is a book designed to be read, front to back, multiple times without you falling asleep.

We'll need IDE's (internal development environments) when we want to try out the code ourselves, but not now.

Contract Creation

We are going to create a new file. This new file will end in '**.sol**'. If you haven't coded before, the extension determines the type of file the system reads it as. The **.sol** extension is used for Solidity files.

It's just like the **.txt** for text files or the **.jpg** for images. All programming languages use their own extensions, like **.html** for html files or **.css** for css.

Mine is going to be called FuckYouAlice.sol.

Also, in case you have ever looked at solidity code and are confused about it - at the top of our file, we'll need to specify the version of Solidity we're using with a *pragma* statement.

This is only there to tell the compiler what version of Solidity to use. If the compiler is the chef, we need to tell it how to cook the recipe we're about to give it with:

```
pragma solidity ^0.8.4;
```

This tells the compiler to use version 0.8.4 - or any newer version that doesn't break functionality (up to, but not including, version 0.9.0). The caret (^) is used to indicate this. It's like saying, *"I want this version or newer, but not so much newer that it's a completely new way of doing things."*

Compiler defined. Next, you'll define your contract.

I liked that chef metaphor so I'll use it again, if pragma was *how* to cook the recipe, then contract is *the recipe*. Here's what it looks like:

```
pragma solidity ^0.8.4;

contract FuckYouAlice {
    // My smart contract goes in here
}
```

This defines a contract named FuckYouAlice, but annoyingly, it does not actually allow me to say fuck you to Alice yet.

The space inside the curly braces ({}) is empty. Soon, it is where we will define what our contract does.

Let's start by defining a *variable* to store our greeting. It's actually known as a **state variable**, because it is available throughout the entire contract, but who cares just yet. This is a variable whose value is permanently stored in contract storage. It's there forever, which is what I want:

string public message;

'Good lord, what the hell is this' I hear you say. *'String? Public?..'*

Remember when we told our contract that our favourite sex position was getting 69'ed? We used *'unit256'*, which specifies a type of data - a number.

(It looked like this: *uint256 FavSexPosition = 69;*)

We are doing the same here. **'string'** is a data type too, it's the data type used for words.

We have a whole section dedicated to variables and data types, so if this goes over your head for now, don't worry, we are doing it quickly so you can look at an actual contract, we'll retrace later.

So, the line of code in order is, firstly:

string

Which defines a variable of data type **string** (words, basically), then:

public

Which is a keyword that means this variable can be read from outside the contract. It's like making your Instagram profile public - and I want *everyone* to see my message to Alice.

message

You can use any variable name here; this is the actual *name* of the 'string variable' that your message is stored in. Therefore, I made the decision to call it 'message'.

I've done this for simplicity's sake, however when writing longer and more complex code - it pays to be very specific. If I were writing a longer contract, I might have called that variable:

rudeMessageToMyExAlice

Great, we defined the name of the variable that can contain our message - but *'where the hell is the actual message? Then?'*

Well, it's not there yet... Sorry.

You've just defined a **string** variable that is **public** that is named 'message'. If you wanted to return the value of that string (what it contains), it would return an empty string, like this: "".

This is because, in Solidity, if you declare a variable but don't assign it a value, it gets initialised with its *default value*. For **string** type variables, the default value is an empty string "".

So, if you declare **string public message;** in Solidity and don't assign it a value, the default value of **message** is an empty string.

The default value for **uint256** in Solidity is **0**. This applies to all unsigned integer types, including **uint256**. So, if we declared:

```
uint256 public bedpostNotches;
```

in Solidity and didn't assign it a value, the default value of 'bedpostNotches' would be **0**. With our earlier example:

```
uint256 favSexPosition = 69;
```

We declared the variable value *right away*; in fact, we could have declared this as:

```
uint256 favSexPosition;
```

But if we had, it would have been initialised at the default value of **0**. This is because we didn't specify a value for the variable to be initialized at.

We are going hard and fast here, and I expect little of this to make sense, but there's a reason we're going very hard very early, stay with me for the hardest bit.

Next, we'll define the value of our **message** variable as soon the contract is deployed. This is high level stuff, using what is known as a 'constructor' and we won't actually be using it till near the end of the book, but it's really handy to know it exists now.

Constructors: Contractual Foreplay

A constructor is a special bit of code that is executed at contract creation *only* - and *cannot* be called afterwards.

Constructors are typically used to create contracts with specific configurations exactly when they are deployed, perhaps to immediately allocate some kind of token balances to accounts - or set the contract *'owner'* right away before someone else does.

They can also be used to perform any other necessary setup tasks when a contract is deployed.

On deployment, for example, you might want to give your personal ETH account one hundred billion $shibashitsu777 tokens. If we were to use one in our contract, it would look like:

```
string public message;

constructor() {
    message = "Fuck you, Alice!";
}
```

This defines a constructor that sets the 'message' variable to "Fuck you, Alice!". This means that as soon as this contract is deployed, our message variable is declared with that particular value.

Now we're ready to use that variable from the get go.

Now I could also define a what is known as a *function* to retrieve this message. A function being a reusable piece of code that performs a specific task. It might look like this:

```
function breakupMessage() public view
returns (string memory) {
    return message;
}
```

This defines a **function** named 'breakupMessage' that returns the 'message' variable. The **public** keyword, as we know, means that this function can be called from outside the contract by anyone - Alice could call this function at 3am after she gets drunk texted.

The **view** keyword is new, it means that this function does not modify the state of the contract - in other words just viewing the message changes nothing in the code, and won't cost you any Ether to do (we will get to this).

The **returns (string memory)** part specifies the data type we want to return - a string. Yeah, it's a little lame we have to specify that, but we do, soon it will be second nature. Honestly.

Don't worry about the **memory** keyword yet.

In reality, we wouldn't need to create a function to view an already **public** function, but this is just to give you an example before we get into visibility options.

Again. I don't expect much of that to make sense yet, but as I said, we're just smashing out a full contract quickly so you can see what one looks like.

Our Full Contract

And there you have it. Our first working contract.

The final touch is something called an SPDX License-Identifier, which we'll chuck in at the top. It's actually a little bit of legal jargon that we aren't going to worry about right now. (Wow, we're really not worrying about a lot right now).

The reason behind the SPDX identifier is that, as all software is viewable on chain, using the MIT License is the most permissible and open-source License there is.

Legality hasn't really adapted to the open source and international waters of smart contracts yet, so sometimes it's better to follow best practices.

So, here's what the *whole thing* looks like:

```
// SPDX-License-Identifier: MIT
pragma solidity ^0.8.4;

contract fuckYouAlice {

    string public message;
```

```
    constructor() {
        message = "Fuck you, Alice!";
    }

    function breakupMessage() public
view returns (string memory) {
        return message;
    }
}
```

This is actually quite a complex contract with that constructor in it, it's a piece of crap, but not quite a piece of shit. So, if you can understand 10% of it - congratulations - rip up that donkey-brain certificate and throw it in the trash.

Now, you might be thinking, *"Alright, I have a piece of code that works, so how do I actually run it?"*.
Well, that's where that 'IDE' comes in.

In reality, a development environment is a bit ahead of us now, seeing as we don't really understand variables yet, but *if you wanted*, you could go to **https://remix.ethereum.org/** right now, and deploy this code on a testnet or mainnet.

All you'd have to do is paste your code into the editor, press a button called compile, and then press a button called deploy.

Then you could call the contract all day to view all the fucks you could possibly want to send Alice.

But for now, pat yourself on the back. You've just written your first Solidity contract. It's a piece of crap, but it's your piece of crap. And that's something to be proud of.

Remember, *'It's not about the destination, it's about the journey. It's about the moments of triumph, the feeling of creating something out of nothing. So, keep going. Keep coding. Keep creating. And most importantly, keep having fun. Because that's what it's all about.'*

I'm sure some overly optimistic wanker has said something almost exactly like that at some point.

Basics Made Easy: Syntax, Comments, and Operators

Before we delve into the nitty-gritty, here is a brief rundown of something taken for granted throughout this book - syntax, comments, and operators.

Anyone who is familiar with programming will know of these already, or at least how they work. For a new learner, within no time at all, these will become second nature. Now, however, they deserve a detailed description to help you understand.

Syntax

Let's talk syntax for a second.

You might know of syntax from a language you know. I think of it as the programming equivalent of English grammar. It's the set of rules that determines how we can or can't write in a particular language. In fact, the word "syntax" comes from the Ancient Greek for "coordination" or "ordering together."

"The dog bit Johnny" conveys a completely different meaning to "Johnny bit the dog". If this happens then you've raised a little nutcase. If you go even further and mess up the order too much then it won't even make any sense.

This is because when you write a sentence in English, you have to follow certain rules, like putting the verb after the subject. Similarly, you can't just tell a computer to "DO THING!" You have to use the right syntax, like:

```
boolean doThing = true;
```

So syntax is the set of rules that defines how you write the code. If you don't follow the rules, the computer won't understand what you're trying to say and your program just won't work. It's like writing a sentence with the words all jumbled up; it doesn't make sense to the reader (or compiler in this case).

For example, in Solidity, a function definition must include the function's visibility (e.g., public or private), its name, its parameters, and its return type. This is because, as we know, Solidity is 'statically typed'.

Comments

Now, comments.

I've already used these; //, a couple of times at the start of a LoC (line of code). Like our SPDX license identifier.

This signifies code that is not going to run, it's just a note on the page to yourself or other developers so they can get an insight into what a bit of code might do. Comments are ignored by the compiler.

In Solidity, you have two types of comments:

- **Single-line Comments**: These start with //. Everything to the right of // on the same line is a comment.

    ```
    // This is a single-line comment in Solidity
    ```

- **Multi-line Comments**: These start with /* and end with */. Everything in between is a comment, even if it spans multiple lines.

    ```
    /* This is a
    multi-line
    comment in Solidity */
    ```

Due to formatting issues, I'm going to use // for all my comments throughout the book, but understand that:

```
/* multi
Line comments do
Exist */
```

Comments are a crucial part of your code. They make it easier for others (and future you) to understand what's going on, especially for complex logic. So, comment your code a lot. I comment religiously, this is because I have somehow managed to master solidity despite being insanely forgetful - so most of my comments are to future me.

This should give you some hope.

Operators

They're just like in school, you probably used mathematical operators like -, +, /, * on your calculator.

Technically, operators are the symbols that tell the compiler to perform specific mathematical or logical manipulations - but there are a few types.

I am going to list them all here, so in the future while reading, you can review back to here if you forget what an operator does.

Here are the types:

Arithmetic Operators:

These are your basic math operators.

+ for addition, - for subtraction, * for multiplication, / for division, and % for modulus (remainder of division).

Modulus might be new if you didn't take advanced math, I did not, so when I started programming it was also new to me.

These operators are your basic tools.

```
uint a = 10 + 5;  // a is now 15, 
because math.
uint b = 10 - 5;  // b is now 5, because 
subtraction.
uint c = 10 * 2;  // c is now 20, 
because multiplication.
uint d = 10 / 2;  // d is now 5, because 
division.
uint e = 10 % 3;  // e is now 1, because 
10 divided by 3 has a remainder of 1.
```

Assignment Operators:

These are the little fellas that let you set your values. = is the most common one, but there are also compound assignment operators like +=, -=, *=, /=, and %=, which do an operation and an assignment in one fell swoop.

```
uint a = 10;  // a is now 10, because we 
just defined it as such.
a += 5;  // a is now 15, because we 
added 5 to what it already was (10).
a -= 5;  // a is now 10 again, because 
we subtracted 5 from it.
a *= 2;  // a is now 20, because we 
doubled what it was (10).
a /= 2;  // a is now 10 again, because 
we halved what it was (20).
```

Comparison Operators:

These (you guessed it) compare things. They take two values and give you what is known as a boolean value, which is a fancy name for 'true or false'.

== checks if two values are equal, != checks if they're not equal, < checks if one is less than the other, > checks if one is greater, <= checks if one is less than or equal, and >= checks if one is greater than or equal.

```
bool a = (10 == 10);  // a is true,
because 10 is indeed equal to 10.
bool b = (10 != 10);  // b is false,
because 10 is not not equal to 10.
bool c = (10 < 20);   // c is true,
because 10 is less than 20.
bool d = (10 > 20);   // d is false,
because 10 is not greater than 20.
```

Logical Operators:

These probably require the most explaining. Logical operators are used to manipulate boolean values too (true or false).

They let you do logical operations for your code to be able to make its own decisions, basically. && is logical AND, || is logical OR, and ! is logical NOT.

```
bool a = (true && true);  // a is true,
because true AND true is true.
bool b = (true || false); // b is true,
because true OR false is true.
bool c = !true;           // c is false,
because NOT true is false.
```

You can always refer back to this page if you see an operator used and aren't familiar with it, but as these operators are the building blocks of your 'contract logic', you will soon not even think twice about what they do.

A Quick Word for Web 2 Devs

(You could skip this if you aren't already a Web 2 developer, but it might give you some insight)

This book is for people new to Solidity and programming in general. However, developers with previous experience will still find this very helpful, and will likely grasp the concepts far faster.

Yet, there are some major differences between traditional programming languages and the EVM, so I'll quickly list the biggest ones here.

The Beauty of Synchronous Programming in Solidity

There's no asynchronous programming here.

You know, that neat trick in JavaScript where your code can multitask? (**Await**, anyone?) Well, Solidity takes a different approach. It's all about doing *one thing at a time*, waiting in line for something to complete before any next action can be taken.

Your code focuses on one task, then moves on to the next, then the next. No distractions, no juggling, just pure, focused, synchronous action. It's a refreshing change of pace that brings simplicity and predictability to your code.

I like it far better, but I'm biased.

State is Your Best Friend

Next, let's chat about state.

In Web 2.0, you're used to having databases to store and manage your application's state. In Solidity, the state is stored on the blockchain. The blockchain is also like the world's best memory - it never forgets.

Every transaction, every change, every action you take is recorded and stored forever. No god damn rollbacks here. This means you can always trace back your steps, audit your actions, and have a clear record of your code's journey. So, embrace the permanence and make it work for you.

Gas Gas Gas!

We mentioned that in the EVM, gas is the energy that powers your code. Every operation, every computation, every transaction costs a certain amount of gas. Gas costs money.

In Web 2.0, you're used to thinking about computational resources in terms of CPU usage or memory allocation. In Solidity, you have to think about gas. But rather than seeing this as a limitation, think of it as a challenge to write efficient, optimised code from the get go.

If your code is a gas-guzzler, it's a sign that you need to refine and improve it. If your code hits *throw;* and the emergency brakes are pulled, you just lost all the gas for that transaction - this can add up for users.

It's not just about getting your code to *work*; it's about getting it to work efficiently so it doesn't cost users millions of dollars to interact with.

External Data: It's a Whole New Ball Game

In the Web 2.0 world, pulling data from external sources is as easy as making an API call.

Need weather data? Hit up a weather API. Need user data from social media? There's an API for that. It's like ordering take away - you ask for what you want, and it gets delivered to you.

In the world of Solidity and the EVM, things aren't so straightforward. The EVM is *deterministic*, meaning it needs to produce the same result every time a function is run. This rules out direct API calls, as the data from an API can change over time.

Oracles: Your Data Delivery Service

This is where oracles come in. In the context of blockchain and smart contracts, an oracle is a service that provides data from the outside world. It's your data courier that delivers to your smart contract.

When your contract needs data, it sends a request to an oracle. The oracle then fetches the data from the external source, and sends it back to your contract. This allows your contract to interact with the outside world, while still maintaining the determinism of the EVM.

However, oracles introduce a new level of trust into the equation. Your contract is now dependent on the oracle to provide accurate and reliable data. It's a matter of trust. I will not go into 'the oracle problem' right now, but basically - when using oracles, it's important to choose reputable providers and to use multiple sources of data when possible, to mitigate the risk (cough cough, Chainlink).

Alright, got that? Let's get started.

'Bitcoin was created to serve a highly political intent, a free and uncensored network where all can participate with equal access.'

– Amir Taaki

Variables, Visibility, and Basic Data Types

Alright, so let's do this.

Quite honestly, a lot of books would have started with fully explaining variables before we got into constructors and contracts. But this ain't your comp sci professor's book. You have now already seen a working solidity contract - even if you understood little of it, it's important. So now we dive into the building blocks of Solidity: variables, types, and memory.

Variables

Variables, in the simplest terms, are like containers for storing data - they're Tupperware. You put something in, you put a lid on it, and you put it in the fridge (or in this case, the blockchain) for later. You can use them at will and they are nicely labelled.

We already know that variables in Solidity are statically typed, too. This means that each variable has a specific data type that we declare when we name our variable. In solidity variables can only hold data of a single type. That Tupperware container, for example, can only hold spaghetti. You try to put in a chicken, and it just won't fit.

There are several data types variables can be in Solidity, we've kind of seen strings (words) and integers (numbers). But let's start with a basic one: boolean types.

Boolean types, or **bool** for short, are used to store (you guessed it) 'Booleans', or rather 'Boolean values'. If you are not a programmer, this will most likely be brand new, but they are simply 'true or false'

Statements. Like a light switch. Either on or off - yes, or No.

Here's what they look like:

bool isPizzaTime;

This declares a boolean variable named 'isPizzaTime'. It can hold the values **true** or **false**. It's simply a yes or no question, is it Pizza time or is it not Pizza time.

When you declare this, you can specify if it is or it isn't pizza time, like:

bool isPizzaTime = true;

However, if you don't specify, like this:

bool isPizzaTime;

Then a **bool** will automatically be **false**. Solidity doesn't think you should be eating pizza right now, sorry.

Okay so boolean values are simple, even if they don't feel like it yet. Now let's go back to Integers (numbers) which we saw but you didn't understand (don't lie).

Integer types, (or **int**) for short, are used to store integer values. These are whole numbers, like 1, 42, or -99. We've seen **uint** used already, which is slightly different.

int = whole numbers either positive or negative.

uint = whole numbers but only positive.

You might (rightly) be thinking; 'Why the fuck would I ever use **uint**, when it's a less capable variable than **int**?' Without getting too much into the weeds, in solidity, it's actually far more common to use **uint**, due to the nature of what the language is used for, I.e., lots of DeFi.

We're going to be using 'uint' for almost everything, briefly, here's why:

- **Non-negative Values**: If you're working with values that can't be negative, such as quantities, distances, or counts (like the number of tokens someone has or the number of votes in a voting contract), then it makes sense to use **uint** to represent these values. Using **uint** can prevent programming errors where a value accidentally goes negative.

- **Efficiency**: Operations with **uint** can be a little bit more gas-efficient (cheaper monetarily) than those with **int**.

- **Larger Positive Range**: **uint** allows for larger positive numbers to be stored compared to **int**. This is because **int** must reserve half of its possible values for negative numbers - there are lots of large numbers in DeFi, as everyone who codes solidity becomes very, very rich.

- **Common Convention**: It's a common convention (a phrase you might begin to hear a lot) in many ERC standards (like ERC-20 and ERC-721) to use **uint** for quantities and identifiers.

In Solidity, you can specify the size of your integer types, from 8 bits to 256 bits. The size of the integer type determines the range of values it can hold. It's like choosing between a small, medium, or large Tupperware container. Here's what it looks like:

```
int8 smallNumber;
int256 bigNumber;
```

This declares two integer variables: 'smallNumber' of type **int8**, and 'bigNumber' of type **int256**. The **int8** type can hold values from -128 to 127, while the **int256** type can hold values from -2^255 to 2^255 - 1. In tupperware terms, **Int8** can hold half an avocado, while **int256** can hold all your lunches for the next week.

(They better not be Pizza, it's not Pizza time yet).

If you decide not to declare your integer size (it's natural to be shy), then Solidity will automatically assume it's 256 – the biggest size. (Thanks Solidity).

Now, you may have seen the '=' operator in the operator section. Here's some examples of using it to assign values to variables:

```
int lifeTheUniverseAndEverything = 42;
uint overNineThousand = 9001;
bool pizzaTime = true;
```

This assigns the value 42 to 'lifeTheUniverseAndEverything', the value 9001 to 'overNineThousand', and the value **true** to 'pizzaTime'. Fuck yeah, it's finally pizza time.

Bear in mind, we did not specify a byte size to these integers, so they will default to 'int256' and 'uint256' respectively.

Now, you might have looked at these variables and wondered where all the other words that you didn't understand went - like **public**. If you actually understood anything in the contract section you might even laugh in superiority, 'he didn't even declare the visibility of his variables! Ha!'.

Firstly, you have a weird laugh, secondly, I didn't use a keyword like **public** or **private**, no, but solidity automatically assigns a visibility to variables if none is declared. They will always default to **private**.

Variable (and Function) Visibility

So, let's talk about this variable visibility. In Solidity, variables can actually be declared in three ways. As **public**, **private** and **internal**. These visibilities decide who has access to the Tupperware that is your variable.

Let's dive into these with a metaphor to guide us before we go all straight edge. Variable types:

- **Public**: Like a drunk uncle at a family gathering. Uncle Public doesn't give a shit who's listening; he'll shout his messages to anyone within earshot. Similarly, public variables and functions are accessible from anywhere, even outside the contract. Solidity even goes the extra mile to whip up what is known as a getter function automatically. (It means you don't need to go to the trouble of making a method of viewing the variable, which is nice of Solidity).

- **Private**: If you had a kinky adult toy that you hid it in your sock drawer. You might even give it a sexy name, like 'private dildoface' (not sexy enough?). Well, nobody's getting a peek at private dildoface except within the contract it's defined in. Not even contracts derived from the one he's in. None of your friends know about private dildoface.

- **Internal**: Internal variables and functions are a little bit like embarrassing family secrets, they aren't as embarrassing as private dildoface, but internal secret is accessible within the contract and its friends (derived contracts) only.

BONUS - External:

These are only for functions, which we will get to shortly, but they are like a post box on your door. They're only meant for those outside the house, if you started posting letters the wrong way out of your door, you'd be a crazy person, which is fine, so are most people that learn to code willingly.

Other contracts and transactions can put mail in this external postbox, but technically the box is still on your turf.

Let's recap.

- **Public:** Functions and variables with this visibility are accessible from within the contract and from other contracts. When you declare a state variable public, Solidity even auto-generates a getter function for it.

- **Private:** If a function or variable is private, it can only be accessed from within the contract it's declared in. Derived contracts aren't privy to these details.

- **Internal:** This visibility type is like a middle ground between public and private. Internal functions and variables can be accessed from within the contract they're declared in and also from contracts that inherit from that contract.

- **External:** Only for functions, but functions of this type can be called from other contracts and transactions, but not from within the contract. These functions can be efficient when dealing with large amounts of data.

Here's what it might look like for the variables:

```
uint256 public unclePublic;
string private privateDildoFace;
bool internal internalSecret
```

Wait a sec, can you see a mistake in this code? Look closely. There is something missing on the end of the **bool** variable declaration.

We haven't covered this yet, but after every statement in your code you need to put a semicolon, like this ";". We've only covered simple statements thus far, but this will make more sense a bit later. Now you won't be able to unsee it.

Anyway, there you have it. Variables. The building blocks of your shitcoins.

Data Types Two: Type Harder

Alright, you've mastered variables and data types!

Actually, about that... There are just a *few* more, and these are the fun ones, I promise.

In Solidity, there are several basic data types that we have already covered, integer types (**int and uint**), boolean types (**bool**), string types (**string**).

There however also address types (**address**), and byte types (**bytes**).

Address

Address types, or **address** for short, are used to store Ethereum addresses. These are 20-byte values that represent the address of an Ethereum account. If you have used Defi before, you have an Eth address already, if you haven't, then it's a little like the postal address of your house. Here's what it looks like in coding action:

```
address public sendToAddressForSecret;
```

This declares a public address variable named **sendToAddressForSecret**. You can assign an Ethereum address to this variable like so:

```
sendToAddressForSecret = 0x2A3f0Cd2E6b7102Fe1b87fA5c8356186955C22C3;
```

This assigns the Ethereum address 0x2A3f0Cd2E6b7102Fc1b87fA5c8356186955C22C3 to the 'sendToAddressForSecret' variable.

Address types have several, cool, built-in functions, too.

This means you can do things with these data types natively that you would normally have to write out a bit of code to do - and if you're becoming a programmer, then you know the number one rule is to be as lazy as possible.

Remember, functions are just bits of code that perform specific tasks, you can name them, just like variables, but we'll get to that later.

Remember when you declared a **public** variable, and solidity automatically gave you a **getter** function, so you could view it easily?

No? Well, it did - it simply means you don't have to write boilerplate code for your variable to be read by the browser or another contract. You'll understand this more when we have to write the code. Addresses have this feature too, though.

For example, with the **address** type, you can use the **balance** function to get the balance of an address like this:

```
uint256 balance = myAddress.balance;
```

But what does it get the balance of **myAddress** in? U.S Dollars? Gold? No, as we mentioned, Ether is measured in *Wei*. It sounds like a Chinese surname, but Wei is the smallest unit of Ether - the fuel that runs Ethereum. Here's a quick rundown of Ether Values, and because it's already **pizzaTime** = **true** we'll continue the theme:

- *Wei*: This is the smallest unit of ether, it's atomic. You can't cut it; the width is smaller than the knife blade. You need 1,000,000,000,000,000,000 Wei to make up 1 Ether.
- Gwei (or GigaWei): You might have used this term if you are in DeFi and you have to set your transaction costs within your wallets manually. It's bigger than a Wei, but still pretty small. You need 1,000,000,000 Gwei to make up 1 Ether. *These are the molecules that make up your pizza.*
- Szabo: Honestly you won't use this term much, I wouldn't worry about it. 1 Ether is 1,000,000 Szabo. *These are the actual crumbs of your pizza.*
- *Finney*: Neither will you use this one. Both Szabo and Finney might be useful terms by the time 2050 rolls around, but not yet. 1 Ether is 1,000 Finney. I'd be pissed if I got 1:1000 slice of pizza, but it's a miniscule slice.
- **Ether**: *The whole motherfuckin' pizza*, don't eat that, it's diet season.

So, apart from Pizza being a terrible metaphor for Ether, we might be able to deduce that:

```
uint256 public balance =
myAddress.balance;
```

Gets the balance of **myAddress** in **wei**, and assigns it to the **balance** variable.

As we've set it as public, we can view the **balance** variable at any time via the built in getter function. That's it. Address types are thankfully very simple.

Bytes

Time for another type.

Next, we have byte types, or **bytes** for short. These are used to store binary data. It's like storing a file on your computer, except it's on *the world's computer!* Here's what it looks like:

```
bytes32 public storeSongLyrics;
```

This declares a public byte variable named 'StoreSongLyrics'. You can assign binary data to this variable like so:

```
storeSongLyrics = "Yeah, yeah, yeah, yeah - Yeah, you fucking with some wet ass pussy - Bring a bucket and a mop for this wet ass pussy - Give me everything you got for this wet ass pussy";
```

This assigns the chorus of Cardi B's 2020 hit, 'WAP', which is a string, to 'StoreSongLyrics'. This horrendous string is *automatically converted* to bytes, because you used the bytes type.

It's akin to saving a document on your computer, a terrible, terrible document.

The cool thing about solidity, as we know, is that deploying this contract on the Ethereum Virtual machine (which is really just a decentralised computer) meaning it's accessible for everyone, forever. Did you know only 1% of ancient literature has survived? Well, now future generations will remember Cardi B's poignant lyrics till the end of human civilisation with none of that worry.

Bravo. Bravo indeed.

Now, you might be wondering, *"What's the difference between **bytes** and **string** types? They both save the data of the message, right?"*

Well, in Solidity, **string** is used to store text data, while **bytes** are used to store raw binary data.

We will get more into this later, but the gist of it is that - just like the difference between a text file and a binary file on your computer - both files could contain just text, but the binary (bytes) file could hold a multitude of other data types.

With the **bytes** type, if you were to store text, it would be all jumbled up into bytecode - while the **string** type would be neatly arranged. **Byte** types can contain images, or *any other data*, however, that **strings** cannot. We only need to know the difference for now, so don't worry too much.

Data Types Three: Type Hardest

You know a couple of minutes ago when I said there were just a few more data types?

I bare faced lied to you.

Honestly, I didn't even feel bad about it, and these ones are probably even harder. You know why? Because I believe in you, $readerName. (Bad programming joke).

I really mean it though, you've come far already, very cool indeed.

I think you can do this. I think you can go the whole nine yards, the full shebang, the entire donkey's shlong. So, in addition to the data types above us, Solidity has a few other data types: **arrays, structs, and mappings.**

Arrays

Arrays are used to store multiple values of the same type. Just like most other programming languages, arrays are defined with square brackets like this [ ].

In solidity, **Arrays** can only hold data of a single type. You can't have an array like this:

```
[1, "two", "three", 4, 5, "six"]
```

Therefore, you define them like this:

```
uint256[] public lotteryNumbers;
```

This declares a public array of integers named 'lotteryNumbers'. You can add values to this array like so:

```
lotteryNumbers.push(42);
```

Yeah, I know, *'what the fuck is this? .push? What does this mean?'*. I'm going to be honest with you. I don't know who made up these names. They sometimes seem really stupid, but to add a new number to an array, you use the words 'push' via what is known as 'dot notation' - I.E you put a little full stop after the variable you want to mess with, and then you can get it to do something with another bit of code known as a function.

Some of these little bits of code are built in, as we saw with:

```
uint256 public balance =
myAddress.balance;
```

With the **.balance** being a built in function of the address type. 'Push' is a built-in function of the array type - there are lots of these to make life easier for programmers. I'll include a cheat sheet at the end of this book, as you don't need to memorise them all.

You can use **.push** to *add* to an array. You simply name the array you want to add to, and then add *.push()*. Inside the brackets goes the **argument** that .push needs to add, like the number 42, if you wanted to add that.

I could go into why it's **.push** to add to an array and **.pop** to take away from an array, but that's complex computer science nonsense that ~~degens will not need~~ no one in their right minds will ever need to know.

A lot of stuff in programming, and solidity in particular, is that you have to learn too much too fast to know the history of everything. You won't be perfect, just memorise what something does and how to use it.

I know programmers who use google for about 80% of their work, you work in an online industry, so use the tools available to you - sticklers that want you to have a photographic memory are usually lying about how much they look up online on a day-to-day basis.

Anyway, we still need to know *how* things work - as we now know, using lotteryNumbers.push(42) adds the value 42 to 'lotteryNumbers'. Do it again and the lotteryNumbers array will **return** [42, 42].

That's basic arrays, essentially *lists of data.*

Structs

Next, we have Structs.

Structs, or structures, are used to group *related variables* together, and this is simpler than it sounds.

Imagine that kinky drawer from before, for sex stuff? Well, I understand (as you're learning programming) it's unlikely to be yours.

I've actually written a book on programming, so there is absolutely *zero chance* that it's mine - but we have to use our imagination here. Here's what it looks like in *struct* form:

```
struct SexDrawer {
    string privateDildoFace;
    bool haveLube;
}

SexDrawer private sexDrawer;
```

This declares a struct named 'SexDrawer' with two fields:

- 'privateDildoFace' of type **string**
- 'haveLube' of type **bool**.

It also declares a public variable named 'sexDrawer' of type **SexDrawer**. Ah man, *'how are there now two sex drawers?'*. How can I declare a variable named *sexDrawer (note the lowercase 's')* of type *SexDrawer (note the uppercase 'S')*.

Literally, the only difference in these names is the first letter being capitalised or not.

Remember that phrase I mentioned earlier? *'Common convention'?*

Well common convention is kind of like the 'manners' of programming, or the unspoken rules. All programmers try to stick by these rules (even though there is no reason for them to, compile-wise) in order to make code more readable between different people.

One of the conventions of solidity follows that of JavaScript (JS for the cool kids), in that it uses what is known as 'camel casing'. Camel casing, just like a camel's humps break up the flat line of its back, utilises capital letters on every new word (except the first). Here's some examples of Camel Casing.

- comeGetSome
- eveningEmissions
- tripToBermunda
- epsteinDidNotKillHimself
- neitherDidJohnMcaffee

Alright you get it, that's camel casing, and we've been using it the whole book thus far. But with structs, we're actually declaring a new *'type'*. That's right, structs are the big boys, they give you the power to create actual data types.

Now, 'common convention', dictates that when we are creating a new data type (a struct) we do not use traditional camel casing - we capitalise the *first letter*, too.

It's also common convention in Solidity to name the new variable **sexDrawer** (camel casing), exactly the same as the data type you created for it, I.e., the data type (or struct) named **SexDrawer** (not camel cased, as it has a capital first letter).

Okay. You now have permission to let your head explode.

I know, it's a lot. This is one you might have to read a few times to get a 50% understanding of, we will go over this later too, but that is the gist of creating structs.

You can, of course, also assign values to the fields of this SexDrawer data type named sexDrawer. When you create sexDrawer it has all the fields you defined in the SexDrawer data type. Using a dot, you can specify the variable within that you would like to change, like so:

```
sexDrawer.privateDildoFace = "rigid,
eight and a half inches, girthy";
sexDrawer.haveLube = true;
```

The dot after sexDrawer specifies what we're actually changing within this particular instance of SexDrawer. Here it's privateDildoFace and haveLube that had default variable values, and the = assignment operator made these variables now contain stuff.

Alright I'm tired of writing sexDrawer. I'm going to explain it in RPG (role playing games, my second WoW reference) terms. If you are using multiple instances of the data type in your contract, you could do it like this; firstly, I create a struct:

```
struct Player {
    string playerName;
    uint256 intelligence;
    uint256 strength;

}
```

Then I add some of those new data types (Player):

```
Player private player1;
Player private player2;
```

I then assign some values to my players:

```
player1.playerName = "Brainiac";
player1.intelligence  = 8;
player1.strength  = 1;

player2.playerName = "Gorlock the
Destroyer";
player2.intelligence  = 1;
player2.strength  = 9;
```

That's structs, they create a type that you can use over and over again, in this case the type is 'Player'. Notice I didn't follow the convention the second time, because I had multiple instances of the struct and used player1 and player2 instead.

Mappings

Okay, I'm not joking here, this is the last data type. I swear.

You might want to recharge; this is heavy intensity stuff if you are brand new to programming.

This last data type is **mappings**. These are used to store what are known as 'key-value pairs'. Key-value pairs are exactly what they say on the tin, just like a dictionary, they map one thing with another.

For example, in the dictionary, the word 'distressing' is one half of a key value pair. It is 'mapped' to its definition:

```
Word: Distressing (noun)
Meaning: Great pain, anxiety, or sorrow;
acute physical or mental suffering;
affliction; trouble.
Or, Cardi B, WAP (Wet Ass Pussy) 2020.
```

In actual code, a **mapping** shakes out like this:

```
mapping(address => uint256) public
addressToNumber;
```

This declares a public mapping named 'addressToNumber' that maps addresses to unsigned integers (gives the address a number). You can assign values to this mapping like so:

```
addressToNumber[0x2A3f0Cd2E6b7102Fe1b87f
A5c8356186955C22C3] = 1;
```

This assigns the value 1 to the key **0x2A3f0Cd2E6b7102Fe1b87fA5c8356186955C22C3** in 'addressToNumber'.

Notice we used [ ] brackets here. What happened when we ran this was that the complier saw we wanted to access the addressToNumber mapping, and we used [ ] to tell it that we had an address inside that we wanted to assign a number to. We then used the assignment operator '=' to map the two together.

It's just like adding a word and its definition to your dictionary.

If we want to go one further, we can use the players example from structs. Say you build a simple game on the blockchain. You would need a way to keep track of each player's character to their **address.** This is because the power of **structs** really shines when you want to create multiple instances.

You could use an **array**, which we covered, like this:

```
Player[] private players;
```

This declares an *array of Player structs*, which you can add to or retrieve from as needed. But mappings are more useful here as we can map **Player** to **address** with ease:

```
mapping(address => Player) private players;
```

This is the same thing as the **address** mapping, except instead of a simple number, it's mapping Player structs. This is useful if you want to associate each player with an Ethereum address.

In these cases, the variable name 'players' is plural to indicate that it can contain multiple Player instances. This is a common naming convention that helps make the code clearer.

The convention you use depends on what you're trying to achieve, and at first, you might make some naming mistakes. At the end of the day, if the code works, it works. Get better at naming things later.

To iterate, though. If you only had one player, **Player private player;** is fine. If you had multiple players, you might use Player[] private players; or mapping(address => Player) private players; instead.

Deep breath.

We made it. Now maybe re-read this for a couple of days in a row and actually get to grips with it. That's usually how learning a new programming language goes.

Data types are all done - along with variables, and you have come a very long way in knowing the DNA of solidity. You even might want to give yourself a pat on the back (what a shite reward) or a cup of tea, or a strong whisky and ten lines of cocaine.

That was some hard stuff, and you nailed it by simply getting this far - and if you didn't understand it all, that's cool, we are going to use all of this as we go. There will be lots more practice.

Onward.

Some Things Never Change: Constants & Immutables

Variables and data types? Smashed it.

Let's meet constants.

In Solidity, constants are variables whose *value cannot be changed* after they are initialised.

Whereas a normal variable is an e-z wipe whiteboard marker, constants are a tattoo, you can't wipe them off and change that photo of a the goatsee guy to something more 'in-law' friendly.

Here's what they look like:

```
uint256 public constant speedOfLight = 186282;
```

This declares a public constant named 'speedOfLight' of type **uint256** and initialises it with the value 186282. Once 'speedOfLight' is initialised, its value cannot be changed.

Constants in Solidity are useful for defining values that *should not* change. They can be any of the data types that we've learned about.

They could be a magic number integral to a game, a configuration setting, or a fundamental constant of the universe. I called my constant 'speedOfLight' because it's a set speed. These constants don't change.

Other, regular variables can be changed at will, like this:

```
uint256 public numberOfBeersConsumed = 6;
```

As you can see, while writing this, I've had 6 beers, if I returned the value of 'numberOfBeersConsumed' I would get the number 6.

However, it's almost 2pm, so I've just cracked another, therefore I need to update my variable.

```
uint256 public numberOfBeersConsumed = 7;
```

With this code, I've just changed my variable. However, with constants, you would not be able to do this once they are set. Solidity would throw an error.

You use constants just like any other variable, though - you can use them in expressions, pass them to functions, return them from functions, (we're almost at functions, hold on!) and so on. It's like using a regular variable, but with the added assurance that the value will never change. It's a guarantee.

For example, you might use a constant to define the maximum supply of a token in a token contract:

```
uint256 public constant MAX_SUPPLY = 
1000000;
```

This declares a public constant named 'MAX_SUPPLY' of type **uint256** and initializes it with the value 1000000. This constant could be used to ensure that the total supply of tokens never exceeds the maximum supply.

It's a hard cap, a limit that cannot be exceeded. In DeFi, this can be important. If you invest $100 into a project, you'd like to be *sure* that the owner can't inflate the supply x10 overnight, making your $100 worth $10.

(Like the traditional monetary system does every single day, but for that, you'd have to read my other book - *Easy Money*. If you have no backing on tradFi, nation states and the role crypto will play in the future, as well as other methods of acquiring capital to invest, check it out).

Anyway, another use case of constants could be to define the version of a contract. Contracts are immutable, so can't be changed in terms of the code - but if variables are not constants they can be updated via the state. By setting a constant version you are telling people, *'I'm not up to any funny business, I won't pretend this version is newer than it actually is at a later date'*.

```
string public constant VERSION = 
"1.0.0";
```

This declares a public constant named 'VERSION' of type **string** and initialises it with the value

"1.0.0". This constant could be used to keep track of the version of the contract.

That's constants! Easy. Used for defining unchangeable values in your code, except it's not the *only* way.

'Immutable' vs 'constant'

In solidity, you have another keyword that defines unchangeable values. **Immutable.**

It's a similar keyword to **constant** but not the same. This is a little complex, as it has a lot to do with optimising gas, but it's good to know both exist.

So, **constants** have these characteristics:

- The value is determined at compile time (when you translate your code into machine readable code). The value must be known and fixed at that time.
- **constant** variables do not take up storage on the blockchain, as they are inlined in the code where they are used.
- They are read-only and cannot be modified. (Duh)

And **Immutables** have these characteristics:

- The value must be assigned in the **constructor** and cannot be changed afterward.
- The value is stored in the contract's bytecode, making it efficient in terms of gas costs.

- Once the contract is deployed, the **immutable** variable becomes read-only and cannot be modified. (Duh).

Here's two examples, first, constants:

```
contract ConstantContract {
    uint256 public constant A_CONSTANT = 1;
}
```

Then, immutables:

```
contract ImmutableContract {
    uint256 public immutable anImmutableValue;

    constructor(uint256 _value) {
        anImmutableValue = _value;
    }
}
```

Okay, so let's look at the comparisons between the two.

Initialisation

- **constant**: Initialized at compile time.
- **immutable**: Initialized in the constructor.

Use Cases

- **constant**: Suitable for fixed values known at compile time, such as mathematical constants.

- **immutable**: Suitable for values that are determined at deployment time, such as configuration parameters.

Best Practices

- Use **constant** for values that are known and fixed at compile time.
- Use **immutable** for values that need to be set at deployment time and remain unchanged throughout the contract's life.

Now you know these two exist, but you probably won't be using them till much later. Just know that both **immutable** and **constant** provide a mechanism to define unchangeable variables, each with its unique characteristics and use cases.

<u>Understanding Scope: Setting Variable Boundaries</u>

In programming, scope refers to *'the region or section of code where a variable or a function is visible and can be accessed'*.

The concept of 'scope' is crucial for maintaining organised code & preventing naming conflicts. In Solidity, state variables are no different from normal variables; they are just defined in the 'global scope', meaning that they are available in all functions.

Here are some examples of state and non-state variables:

```solidity
pragma solidity ^0.8.6;

contract Global {
    uint public globalVar = 100;

    function weStillHaventCoveredFunctions() public view returns(uint) {
        // Inside is a local variable, only accessible within this function.
        uint localVar = 200;
        return localVar + globalVar;
    }
}
```

In this example, you can see that as soon as we've named our contract, we defined this:

```solidity
uint public globalVar = 100;
```

This is a state variable that is accessible from all functions within the Global contract. It's stored in the blockchain itself, so its value persists between function calls.

On the other hand, 'localVar' is a local variable. This is only accessible within the 'weStillHaventCoveredFunctions' **function**. It's stored in memory (which is basically short-term memory), so its value does not persist between function calls.

When 'weStillHaventCoveredFunctions' is called, it returns the sum of 'localVar' and 'globalVar' (300). If you tried to access 'localVar' in another **function**, you wouldn't be able to.

It's important to note that in Solidity, the term global variables also refers to special variables and functions which are globally accessible and provide information about the blockchain or utility functions.

Examples include **block.timestamp** (which provides the current block timestamp) and **msg.sender** (provides the address of the caller of the current function). However, these are not the same as state variables as they are available in all contracts inherently and do not need to be defined.

These built-in global variables are always there, like the laws of physics, always governing how things work. Use them like this:

```
uint256 public currentTime = block.timestamp;
```

This assigns the timestamp of the current block to the public global variable 'currentTime'. The equivalent of checking your watch and writing down the time.

Then there's **msg.sender**, which gives you the address of the sender of the current function call. It's Solidity's caller ID, it shows you exactly who's sending that transaction. It's useful because you can use it to shortcut assign anything to the person sending the transaction - like assigning **msg.sender** a player character:

```
players[msg.sender] = newPlayer;
```

A simplified version would be to simply create an address type, name it 'sender', and assign the address of **msg.sender** to it:

```
address public sender = msg.sender;
```

This assigns the address of the sender of the current function call to the public global variable **sender**.

There's also a **msg.value**, which gives you the amount of Ether sent with the current function call. In code, it's:

```
uint256 public value = msg.value;
```

So, this assigns the amount of Ether sent with the current function call to the public global variable **value**.

Wow, we're really humming along now. I know it's getting a little hard, but we're actually going to peak in difficulty early - in fact, the hardest stuff is probably understanding memory in Solidity. This is because it's a relatively new concept in programming, and isn't really important in Web2.

So, grab a fresh beverage (that reminds me: **uint256 public numberOfBeersConsumed = 8;**) and let's continue on.

Prefixes: Code Nicknames

Now we actually know what variables are, we can have a quick look at 'naming conventions'.

Naming conventions are yet another example of 'best practice' or 'common convention' - in that the contract will compile fine without them.

They only play a role in making the code more 'human readable' for both you and others. This is because common prefixes can provide more context on the nature and intended use of that variable.

Here are some common prefixes, (or methods of naming variables) used in Solidity. You *do not have to use these*. In fact, I haven't been using them throughout the explainers, as it's another layer of complexity that you don't really need in your first contracts.

However, if you want to follow 'best practice' or need to read complex code, these prefixes may be included.

1. State Variables (s_)

- **Prefix:** s_
- **Indicates:** A state variable, which is stored on the blockchain.
- **Example:**

    ```
    uint256 private s_balance;
    ```

2. Immutable State Variables (i_)

- **Prefix:** i_
- **Indicates:** An immutable state variable, which can only be set once in the constructor.
- **Example:**

   ```
   address private immutable i_owner;
   ```

3. Local Variables & Function Parameters (_)

- **Prefix:** _
- **Indicates:** A local variable, which is only accessible within the function where it is declared.
- **Examples:**

   ```
   function setBalance(uint256 _balance) public { s_balance = _balance; }
   ```

4. Global Variables (g_)

- **Prefix:** g_
- **Indicates:** A global variable that might be used across different functions or even different contracts.
- **Example:**

   ```
   uint256 public g_totalSupply;
   ```

5. Constants (c_)

- **Prefix:** c_ or simply USE_ALL_CAPS
- **Indicates:** A constant value that is known at compile time and will not change.
- **Example:**

```
uint256 public constant c_maxSupply =
1000000;

uint256 public constant MAX_SUPPLY =
1000000;
```

As mentioned, these prefixes only offer a way to convey additional information about variables, it is not mandatory to use them.

You don't have to use them, and you'll likely forget sometimes, but it's a whole lot easier if you do.

That said, conventions do change, even between projects and teams, so these aren't set in stone. They are good to be aware of though in order to adapt as needed.

Storage & Memory: Big Brain Not Needed

Alright, you've grappled with variables, data types, constants, and global and state variables. I still think those sections need to be read a couple of times to fully grasp – but if you have, you're now looking like a pro. Now it's time to delve into storage and memory.

In Solidity, there are two places where you can store data, and like the title of this chapter, they are:

- Storage.
- Memory.

One of these, **storage**, can be looked at like a storage unit. For this chapter, let's imagine you rent a storage unit yourself, because it's down the road from your house.

You put things in this unit, unsurprisingly, for long-term storage. The unit is only for things that you don't need every day. You store your shorts and sandals during the winter, or Christmas decorations all year until it hits December.

You wouldn't, however, store your friend's dog Spot in the storage unit. He might stay in the living room for a bit while you have a cup of tea, but he's just passing through.

Memory is like the living room of your code, *in then out*, it doesn't need to store anything long term.

Storage is where all the contract state variables reside, it's a storage unit, it costs more (in gas) but once you put something in storage, it stays there. At least until you explicitly remove or change it. Here's what it looks like:

```
uint256 public thisIsPutInStorage = 777;
```

This declares a public state variable named **thisIsPutInStorage** of type **uint256** and initializes it with the value 777. **thisIsPutInStorage** is put in storage - therefore it persists. Just like putting your Christmas decorations in a box in the storage unit - they stay there until you need them.

Memory, on the other hand, is just a temporary place to store data. Like your friend's dog visiting just for an hour, it doesn't stick around. Anything you put in memory will disappear at the end of the function call. It looks like this:

```
function friendVisits() public {
    uint256 timeSpotWasHere = 1;
}
```

This declares a local variable named 'timeSpotWasHere' inside the function 'friendVisits' and initializes it with the value 1. 'timeSpotWasHere' is stored in memory and only exists during the execution of the function. Spot was only in the living room for an hour; when your friend left, he didn't need to be looked after anymore.

Now, the question here is; "*When should I use storage, and when should I use memory?*" And of course, it depends on what you're trying to do.

Clearly, if you are working with data that needs to 'persist' or stick around in between your function calls, you would use **storage**. This could be a general state variable, a contract balance, a user's account information, or something else. Like I said, it's just like storing your winter clothes away for summer - you don't need them right now, but you will need them when winter hits. You might not need the contract balance for every function call, but you need it to stick around permanently to keep track of it.

On the other hand, if you're working with data that only needs to exist during a function call, just use **memory**. This could be a temporary variable within the function - like a small calculation result, it could be a function argument (data that goes into a function, to be used within it (covered in the next section) or a returned value you only need once.

You might ask; *'Okay, so why wouldn't I stick everything in storage, just in case?'*.

Because that storage unit costs you money.

The more you put in it, the more you're gonna have to pay, as the owner 'upgrades' your package to more square footage.

As we've mentioned, transactions on the Ethereum blockchain use 'gas' which is measured in Ether, which can eat up your user funds quickly if not optimized. Everything in storage will cost gas when interacted with - so best practice is to minimize everything that is put into storage within your contract - use memory if you can!

Next stop, (finally!), functions.

'Gradually, decentralized trust will be accepted as a new and effective trust model. We have seen this evolution of understanding before — on the Internet.'

- **Andreas Antonopoulos**

Making things Happen: Functions

Should we have spent this long before we got to functions? The little bits of code that programming is *actually* all about?

Yes.

I assure you, the backing we have already will serve you far better now than if we had started here. Functions weave spells within your code, they are the bits of it that actually *makes things happen*. So, let's get started.

In Solidity, like other programming languages, functions are defined as blocks of code that perform a specific task. They can be called over and over once defined.

Spells in Harry Potter are a bit like functions, you say the incantation, and the spell happens:

```
function avadaKedavra() public {
    // insert code that kills people
}

// cast it like this:
avadaKedavra();
```

That's right there is a function.

This declares a function named 'avadaKedavra'. When 'avadaKedavra' is called, it executes the code inside the squiggly brackets '{}', this code would be some dark wizard shit.

Now, let's break down the parts of a function. Firstly, there's the function keyword. You can see it right at the beginning of that first line of code. This tells Solidity that you're defining a **function**, not a **uint** or **string**.

Next comes the function name, 'avadaKedavra', in this case. This is what you decide to call the function. It's *naming* the spell that you will be casting in the future, perhaps again and again.

On the end of this 'avadaKedavra' name, there are two brackets () with nothing inside them. This is normal, and in more complex functions you will put parameters inside these to use within your functions, in this case you'd probably put in the name of the witch or wizard you want to waste, but that comes later.

Next, there's function visibility. We've covered this, but it determines *who* can call the function - who can cast this particular spell. In this case, the function visibility is **public**, which means anyone can call the function. (But they have to really *mean* it).

Finally, there's the function body. Which starts at the first squiggly bracket '{'.

This is where you write the code that gets executed when the function is called. It's what goes into the spell. In this case, the function body is empty, so let's give an example of some code you might have in there - even if it's completely useless:

```
function avadaKedavra() public {

    // Check if the sender is a dark
wizard. Only dark wizards can use Avada
Kedavra. Let's use Voldemort.
    require(msg.sender == Voldemort,
"Only dark wizards can use Avada
Kedavra!");

    // Find the target player. For this
example, let's say it's Harry.
    Player memory harry =
players[harryAddress];

    // Check if Harry has a protection
spell active.
    if (harry.hasProtectionSpell) {

        // If he does, the spell fails
and Voldemort loses some power.
        voldemort.power -= 10;
        emit SpellFailed("Avada Kedavra
failed because Harry has a protection
spell active!");
    } else {

        // If not, Harry is fucked.
        delete players[harryAddress];
        emit PlayerKilled("Harry has
been killed by Voldemort's Avada
Kedavra!");
    }
}
```

There is a whole lot of stuff here that you don't to understand yet - but I've sneakily put in a lot of advanced concepts. All you have to worry about, however, is that this is a function *with code in it that does stuff.*

So, you have a working spell! But we've only written out how it works, not how we would *cast* it, so *"How do I call a function (or cast my spells)?".*

Easy. You just use the function name, followed by parentheses. Like this:

```
avadaKedavra();
```

This calls the function 'avadaKedavra'. You said the magic words, and the spell is cast. Alright, simple enough. Now let's level up and talk about these: '()'

Functions can do more than just perform actions on their own. They can also take inputs and return outputs. If the target of your spell comes from outside data, like human input or another contract - you can specify it here. The complicated version might look like this:

```
function avadaKedavra(address _targetAddress) public {

    // Check if the sender is a dark wizard. Only dark wizards can use Avada Kedavra. Let's use Voldemort.
    require(msg.sender == Voldemort, "Only dark wizards can use Avada Kedavra!");
```

```
    // Find the target player using the
provided address.
    Player memory target =
players[_targetAddress];

    // Check if the target has a
protection spell active.
    if (target.hasProtectionSpell) {

        // If they do, the spell fails
and Voldemort loses some power.
        voldemort.power -= 10;
        emit SpellFailed("Avada Kedavra
failed because the target has a
protection spell active!");
    } else {

        // target is blown away
        delete players[_targetAddress];
        emit PlayerKilled("The target
has been killed by Voldemort's Avada
Kedavra!");
    }
}
```

In all probability, this piece of code will make 0 sense to you. All you need to concentrate on for now, however, is this line:

```
function avadaKedavra(address
_targetAddress) public
```

This declares a function named 'avadaKedavra' that takes an input, _targetAddress, and if the person calling it is a dark wizard, deletes the target. _targetAddress can come from anywhere, the function is

public so anyone could call it — (but it would only work if they are pass the check and are a dark wizard, in this case Voldemort).

It's a lot, but you got the gist - functions do things.

Function Modifiers

In Solidity, function modifiers are used to change the behaviour of functions. You add a modifier to a function, and it will change how the function works.

In DeFi, these are tremendously important, as tweaks that change how your functions behave can put limits on what they do and who can use them. Here's an example:

```
modifier onlyOwner {
    require(msg.sender == owner, "Not the owner!");
    _;
}

function doSomethingBad() public onlyOwner {
    // Now this can only be called by the contract owner!
}
```

This declares a function modifier named **onlyOwner** and a function named **doSomethingBad** that uses the **onlyOwner** modifier. The **onlyOwner** modifier checks if **msg.sender** is equal to **owner** and reverts the transaction if it's not.

Think about how important this might be for a second. Everything is on chain and viewable in a smart contract. If a function deals with funds, the person deploying it might want to make sure they are the only person who can call it. With the **onlyOwner** modifier, the function will only work for the owner.

As you can see, that's only a small bit of code - and the cool thing is that modifiers can be used over and over again once defined.

Defining a modifier is easy, too.

First, as we can see, there's the modifier keyword. This tells Solidity, just like with a function keyword, what you are defining. Here you are defining a modifier.

Next, and same as functions, there's the name. This is what you want to call the modifier. In this case, the modifier name is **onlyOwner.**

Then, there's the modifier body, again this goes inside the squiggly bracket '{'. This is where you write the code that gets executed when the modifier is used. In this case, the modifier body checks if **msg.sender** is equal to **owner.** It reverts the transaction if it's not.

Finally, there's the underscore.

_;

This is actually where a function *will be inserted* if you use this modifier on it.

Notice the underscore (that will become the function) is at *the end* of the modifier, this is so the function body gets executed *after* the modifier.

```
modifier onlyOwner {
    require(msg.sender == owner, "Not the owner!");

    // now we have the underscore - which is where the function this modifier will be used on gets executed:

    _;

}
```

We will play with Function modifiers more later - where we can import entire libraries with pre-made modifiers for us to use without having to go through the bother of defining them ourselves. For now, let's move onto the results of our functions - return variables.

Getting Answers: Return Variables

In Solidity, like other languages, functions can **return** values. They'd be pretty useless if they didn't, **return** is how you get the results of any computation you've been doing within a function. Here's a basic Solidity function:

```
function crazyHot(uint256 hotness,
uint256 craziness) public returns
(uint256) {
    uint256 result = hotness -
craziness;
    return result;
}
```

This declares a function named 'crazyHot' that takes two inputs, 'hotness' and 'craziness'. It then subtracts the number 'craziness' from that of 'hotness', and returns the result.

Let's quickly revisit memory here. 'result' is a temporary local variable in **memory** (not storage). You only need this variable for a second, to get your answer. You don't need to put it in storage.

Back to 'crazyHot'. If we were working on a scale of 0-10, I personally wouldn't date any chick who passed into this function with a **result** of less than 7. If you've seen me on a night out and thought differently, that was because it was a trick of the light, or a one-time thing. Multiple, one-time things. So, we really want to store our result somewhere, so we can compare all the chicks later.

Now, let's break down the parts of this important function and **return** statement. We know the start of defining the function by now; we let the compiler know this is a function, named it, defined the parameters and what data type they are, and we also made it public:

```
function crazyHot(uint256 hotness,
uint256 craziness) public returns
(unit256)
```

So, let's start from the **return** keyword.

return tells Solidity that you actually want to get something from all that computation you entered, in this case 'returns (**uint256**)' means that you've specified this function returns a value of **uint256**.

If you don't actually ask the function to return anything, it won't. Other high level programming languages may not need you to enter this, they often just assume that you want to get a result after asking the function to compute something - which is a fair assumption - but Solidity does not.

Not **return**ing anything in Solidity is kind of like turning on your PlayStation (which is engaging in lots of computational power to run Call of Duty) but forgetting to turn on the T.V. It's still doing all that computation; you just can't see it or interact with it.

The function then goes on to be defined as normal, in that we now input what computation we would like it to run.

```
uint256 result = hotness - craziness;
```

Now we've defined a **uint256** as 'result', which is the product of the computation of the two parameters (technically now known as arguments, but most degens and seasoned coders use those terms interchangeably).

This 'result' is going to be our return value, or what we actually want to get out of this function so we know if going on a date with them will be worthwhile. So, the next line is simply:

```
return result;
```

Great, this is now a fully functioning... function? In other words, it works.

So now let's find out who is date-able. We are going to do a 'function call' (we're going to use our newly defined function) to 'crazyHot' and get us a return value:

```
uint256 becca = crazyHot(9, 8);
```

This calls the function 'crazyHot' with the arguments 9 (becca is smoking hot) and 8 (she's also been known to cut up her boyfriend's clothes and has a ketamine addiction).

This stores **becca** as a 1. Why?

Well because we used '9' as the input for 'hotness', and '8' as the input for 'craziness'. Our function created a variable called 'result' and stored 'hotness – craziness' (or '9 – 8'). It then returned 'result', which we stored as 'becca'.

Or put simply, do not date 'becca'.

We could go one further and store 'becca', along with some other potential partners into an array, so we'll do that, it'll be a good refresher and allow us to know who to hit on.

We know basic arrays, they use the brackets that look like this, '[ ]'. Ironically, those who use Tinder (I don't, as the app would break with the amount of likes I'd get) will likely have their matches stored in some kind of array. They are a list, but instead of seeing faces, the code sees hard numbers.

Time for an interesting way to navigate return variables and functions. Let's say that we add an array, stored within **storage**, to our contract. As we know, this means it's always there and not just transient, it can go anywhere in the contract that's outside a function as it's a state variable.

```
uint256[] public potentialDates;
```

Here we've created a **potentialDates[ ]** array as a state variable. Again, this could be put anywhere, but it's usually put at the start of the contract so you can keep track of all your state variables.

Remember in Solidity an array can't handle multiple data types. So, we started by telling Solidity what kind of array to create - a **uint256**.

It's **public**, too, just like me and Becca's break up (I still miss that jacket). Next, we named the array 'potentialDates'.

Now you have to fill that array with some top broads or disaster dates.

```
potentialDates[0] = crazyHot(9, 8); //
Becca, a hot psychopath
potentialDates[1] = crazyHot(3, 0); //
Sarah, friend zoned
potentialDates[2] = crazyHot(8, 1); //
Hannah, definitely doable
```

Notice that we're using '[ ]' to select a *location within this array.*

In programming, ten different numbers would be 0 to 9. Confusing? Yeah.

It just means that counting in programming doesn't start at 1, it starts at 0. The *first* thing you store in an array is at location [0], not at location [1]. Location [1] is the second element in that array.

So, again - 0 is always included as a position within an array, it's the first slot. By selecting 'potentialDates[0]', we are selecting the first position in this array so that we can store something in it.

We did this by assigning the product of 'crazyHot(9, 8)' to it.

Now, this wouldn't actually assign a name to that position, it's only going to the resultant numbers of each equation.

As a side note - if you are a girl doing these functions, you could just replace the hot/crazy matrix with: *'money' vs 'dick size'* - this will make the function just as objectifying and you should feel nice and empowered.

Now here's a question, if we defined it like this:

```
uint256[3];
```

Then could we put any more numbers into this array?

I think you might be able to guess this.

Ready?

The answer is no. You could only put three numbers into this array.

This way of defining an array means it is not a 'dynamic array', it won't expand past the number you defined it to hold, in this case, three. If you wanted to input more numbers into this array you couldn't – it's defined as a 'static array' that holds just three values.

Enough on recapping arrays, let's look at another way functions can impact your code.

If you want to get something out of a function you can use the **return** keyword we just looked at. However, functions can still effect changes when you run them, for examples they can edit state variables and more without having to **return** anything.

Functions can also run other functions! Which sounds complicated but it really isn't. In traditional programming this is known as a 'callback function'.

Let's try it, here's a long bit of code, can you see what each bit is doing?

```
uint256[] public potentialDates;


function crazyHot(uint256 hotness,
uint256 craziness) public returns
(uint256) {
    uint256 result = hotness - craziness;
    return result;
}


function storePotentialDates() public {
    potentialDates.push(crazyHot(9, 8));
// Becca, a hot psychopath
```

```
    potentialDates.push(crazyHot(3, 0));
// Sarah, friend zoned
    potentialDates.push(crazyHot(8, 1));
// Hannah, definitely doable
}
```

It may look complicated, but you actually know everything that this code is doing!

First, we stored a state variable called 'potentialDates' as a **unit256 array**. It's empty, but we can fill it up later.

Secondly, we defined our 'crazyHot' function, which we just explained. It takes away the crazy score from the hot score.

Now here's the new part; we created a new function to store values to our array!

The function is called 'storePotentialDates', and it doesn't actually **return** anything, it just pushes results to our array and changes *that*.

It does it with this:

potentialDates.push(crazyHot(9, 8));

Here we've used **potentialDates.push** to push a value to our array. But what is the value? Well, the value is the result of 'crazyHot()' with the values 9 and 8 as inputs.

This means the function edited our contract by storing the 'result' that 'crazyHot' would **return** to it inside a state variable.

We also know that **.push** just adds a value to an array, so each value **.push**ed will come after the next.

So, there you have it. Return variables - the results of your functions. You'll be defining a lot of them, as we're now starting to get to the part where your code *actually does stuff*. Cool Right?

Let's take a more in-depth look at methods of calling these functions so we can get these return variables and do more with them. Maybe even inserting them into the arguments of other functions!

On Dial:
Calling Functions and Handling Missed Calls

Remember when I mentioned smart contracts were their own autonomous agents living on the blockchain, doing their thing once deployed?

Well, it's possible to interact with these in a few different ways.

The first way is to simply interact with one from an externally owned address, like your own private wallet (shortened to EOA in smart contract land). This could be as basic as you sending a transaction with some data inside it that calls a function, like the **breakupMessage()** from our first contract.

Contracts (and the functions within them) can also be interacted with from another contract address (shortened to CA usually), this is a contract calling another contract - but we're not going to go over that yet as 'contract to contract' is a bit more complex. All you need to know is that in EVM land, every interaction starts from a user or EOA address, after this, a chain reaction can occur in which contracts call other contracts.

Okay, so when sending data to (or calling) a contract, what if something went wrong, or there was user error? Like for example if you called a function within a contract that didn't exist?

That's where fallback functions come in. Fallback

functions are safety nets - designed to catch anything that falls through the cracks of your code.

A fallback function gets called when no other function matches the function signature, or if no data is supplied to the call:

```
fallback() external payable {
    // I got you bro, I'll trigger if the contract is called with no data, or the wrong data
}
```

These will sit in your code in the case of the 'what ifs' and defining them is simple.

First, there's the **fallback** keyword. We haven't put any parameters in between the () here. This is because you don't need to; fallback functions *do not take parameters.* In Solidity 0.6.0 and later, which you will be using, there are two types of fallback functions:

- fallback()
- receive()

They *both* do not take parameters and work in very similar ways.

- The fallback() function is triggered when a call to the contract does not call to any function that is in the contract - or if no data is supplied at all.

- The receive() function is triggered when a call to the contract is made with empty calldata and non-zero Ether. (Someone sent you money).

Here's an example of a receive() function:

```
receive() external payable {
    // I get executed when a call is made with empty calldata and 'non-zero Ether'. Have you ever heard of a more needlessly complex term than 'non-zero ether'?

Seriously, that's how it's described in the Eth docs. Stupid. Just say, 'some Ether'.

I'm still doing this in the code block, aren't I?

You know what, I don't care. Non-zero Ether is a silly way to phrase it…

}
```

Anyway, back to it.

These two functions are also limited in how much gas they can possibly use, so don't go writing a huge function body in there - complex operations should be avoided.

So, these two are quite easily defined, but might not be of much use till you are coding more complex contracts. But it's good to know they exist.

Do notice, too, that the fallback functions can only be called from *outside* the contract, hence the **external** keyword. This makes sense, as they are meant to be called when a call to the contract doesn't match any other function, or when Ether is sent to the contract, which are both things that happen from outside the contract. Now, you might be thinking, *"I kind of get it, but when would I use these bad boys?"*

Well, one common use case is to create a contract that can receive Ether. Here's what it looks like:

```
fallback() external payable {
    emit Received(msg.sender, msg.value);
}
```

This declares a fallback function that emits an event named 'Received' when the contract receives Ether. The Received event takes two parameters:

- msg.sender
- msg.value

msg.sender, as we have seen, is a special global method in Solidity that contains the address of the person (or contract) who triggered the current function.

msg.value, as we have also seen, is another special method that contains the amount of Ether (in wei) sent with the message.

So, when someone sends Ether to the contract without calling a specific function, this fallback function will be triggered. It will then **emit** an **event** (both of these are keywords) with the sender's address and the amount of Ether sent. This can be useful for tracking and verifying transactions. We haven't got to **emit** yet, but it's coming soon.

So, there you have it. Fallback functions, each contract can have **one receive** function and **one** fallback function. Fallbacks are good if your contract is expected to interact with other contracts that might mistakenly send Ether or call non-existent functions, it'll make sure your contract doesn't fail unexpectedly.

Especially in future, when interactions you might not have anticipated might come into effect, a fallback could handle these without breaking functionality of the contract. Good to know they exist!

Snap Necks, Cash Checks: Payable, Solidity's Coolest Keyword

One of the best features of Solidity is that you can send money permissionlessly across the globe in seconds. In your smart contracts, you can make your functions able to receive Ether using the coolest keyword there is.

The **payable** keyword.

We just saw this one sneak into those fallback functions, as **fallback** and **receive** both need to be **external** and **payable** for someone to be able to send Ether to them.

So **payable** is used to allow a function (or of course our fallback functions) to receive Ether. Pretty essential if your smart contract deals with financial transactions on the EVM.

```
pragma solidity ^0.8.0;

contract FuckYouPayMe {

    function pay() public payable {
        // Accepts Ether! Now go find some people to pay you!
    }
}
```

In the above example, the 'FuckYouPayMe' **function** is marked as **payable**, allowing it to accept Ether when called.

Receiving Ether

When a **payable** function is called, the value sent with the call is accessible through the **msg.value** global variable. It's another built in value like **msg.sender** we've looked at. This value is in wei, the smallest unit of Ether:

```
pragma solidity ^0.8.0;

contract FuckYouPayMe {
    uint256 public totalDonations;

    function pay() public payable {
        totalDonations += msg.value;
// That code increments the total donations by the sent value, while still receiving and keeping the Ether
    }
}
```

In this example, the pay function increments the **totalDonations** state variable by the value sent with the call.

Transferring Ether

A contract can transfer Ether to an address using the **transfer** or **call** method on an address marked as **payable**. Here's an example of the full contract, allowing you as an owner of the contract to withdraw all that sweet, sweet Ether whenever you'd like.

```solidity
// SPDX-License-Identifier: MIT
pragma solidity ^0.8.4;

contract FuckYouPayMe {
    uint256 public totalDonations;
    address public owner;

    // Constructor to set the contract deployer (us) as the owner
    constructor() {
        owner = msg.sender;
    }

    function pay() public payable {
        totalDonations += msg.value;
    }

    // Withdraw function to allow the owner to withdraw all the juicy Ether from the contract
    function withdraw() public {
        require(msg.sender == owner, "Only the contract owner can withdraw, get out of here");

payable(owner).transfer(address(this).balance);
    }
}
```

In the above example, we use some more dot notation for the **withdraw** function. Specifically, this line:

```solidity
payable(owner).transfer(address(this).balance);
```

As we're getting a bit more used to Solidity now, let's tackle this pretty complex line. In order to do so, let's further break it down:

address(this).balance:

'address(this)' refers to the address of the current contract. By wrapping 'this' in the brackets you're converting 'this contract' into an address type.

We also know we can do dot notation to get properties like msg.sender, so here we're simply doing it to get **address.balance.** It's going to return us the amount of Ether (in wei).

Together it's 'address(this).balance', and it gets the current balance of the contract in wei. So, what does **payable(owner)** mean?

The **owner** variable we know, as we made it a state variable, using a constructor to hold the Ethereum address of the contract's owner. Next, **payable(owner),** is a little more complex. In Solidity, **address** types have two subtypes:

- address
- **address payable**

The best way to think about it is that even if the address you are trying to send to *can always receive Ether* (like your own EOA wallet) you still have to explicitly state it can while defining their address in your own code.

Just like if you forget to add the '**payable**' keyword to a **function**, you'd find no Ether would be able to be sent to it, and it will revert.

In the same vein, only **address payable** types can use the .transfer() and .send() methods.

So, the **payable()** function is used to explicitly cast an **address** to an **address payable**. So, **payable(owner)** ensures that the **owner** address can receive Ether.

Cool. Let's join the two up.

.**transfer()** is a method available on **address payable** types. It's used to send Ether from the current contract to another address. The amount of Ether to be sent is specified in wei as the argument to the .**transfer()** method – this means in the argument we're putting the whole bank, or '**address(this).balance**'. This means we're transferring the whole kitty.

If the transfer fails for any reason, (for example, due to a gas issue), the entire transaction will revert. Let's put it all together now!

```
payable(owner).transfer(address(this).balance);
```

So, this sends the *entire balance* of the contract to the 'owner' address.

If the transfer is successful, the contract sending the balance will be zero after this line executes. If the transfer fails, the transaction will revert and no Ether will be sent.

'To master a new technology, you have to play with it.'
   - Jordan Peterson

If, Else, and the Art of Decision Making

All **gas**, no steering (get it? Because EVM computation runs on gas?).

Tough crowd.

Well, without a control structure, your contract will act like that. In Solidity, control structures are steering wheels. Tools that let you control the flow of *how* your code is executed.

If you aren't new to programming you will know of *if/else* statements. If you are new, then also great, *if/else* statements are very human readable. (Unlike some of the code we just looked at). Basically, they act how they read. *if and else* statements help your code be more dynamic. Here's a basic and non-fun example to drive it home.

```
if (condition) {
  // This code will execute if the condition is true
} else {
  // This code will execute if the condition is false
}
```

Quite simple really:

- *The condition is true?* Execute the code in the first 'if' block.
- *The condition is false?* Execute the code in the second 'else' block instead.

Anakin just got knighted as Darth Vader? *Execute order 66.*

if/else statements work as *basic decision makers.* As an example, let's say you drive to work and you can take the short suburban route or the longer motorway route. Usually, you take the suburban route, unless there's roadworks or heavy traffic, then you take the motorway as it's more reliable.

You have a basic decision structure here; you check the route and: **'if'** route is free from obstructions then take the usual route. **'Else'** take the longer route.

Your contract can do this too.

The parts of an *if/else* statement are simple enough. As you can see, first there's the *if* keyword. This tells Solidity that you are starting a statement to make a decision.

Next, there's the 'condition' on what puts that decision into action. For now, the condition is just a placeholder, but it could be any expression that evaluates to a boolean. (A truthy or falsy value, or 'true' or 'false' remember?).

Simple enough. The 'else' block also does what it says on the tin. It gets executed if the condition is false.

"So when would I use an if-else statement?"

Well, one common use case is to check a condition and execute different code depending on the result.

```
if (msg.value > 1 ether) {
    // Here we put code to accept this amount and send out something in return
} else {
    // Here we put code to reject this amount, it's not enough!
}
```

You might want to use a similar statement if you were doing an old school ICO - where people send in Ether and you give a token out in return. Or if you were writing an NFT platform for example, one that needed the msg.value to be over the asking price to accept.

So, there you have it. *If and else.* They're the art of decision making in Solidity, the switches on your train tracks. They're a powerful tool for controlling the flow of execution. Onto loops.

Loops: Why Do Something Once, When You Can Do It a Trillion Times

Loops are repetitions in your code.

They are tools that let you cycle an action multiple times.

Let's say you put a hamster on a manually controlled wheel. You then set this wheel to run 10 turns, meaning it will rotate one full cycle 10 times.

That's fine, unless you fuck up and accidentally forget to put the conditional of '10 times' in there, meaning the wheel keeps turning forever. This is what is known as an infinite loop.

If this happens, the hamster will run until its tiny legs fall off and it dies, so make sure you specify loops properly, like this:

```
for (uint i = 0; i < 10; i++) {
    // Mr. Hammy runs one loop of the wheel!
}
```

This declares a 'for loop' that repeats the code in the loop body (running one loop of the wheel) 10 times. It put Mr. Hammy on a wheel and made him run just 10 laps.

I know this code looks quite mathsy and complicated, so let's say you didn't set any conditions within your *'for'* loop. So, instead of these parameters:

for (uint i = 0; i < 10; i++)

You'd have this:

for (;;) // Inside are no conditions, just the ;; syntax you need for a loop.

Maybe you maybe you're trying to power your Tesla with rodent energy, or trying to invent perpetual motion? I dig it. It won't work, though. Normally in programming languages this would throw an error on compilation, or - if run - crash the program.

Still, if you really want to give Mr. Hammy the workout of his tiny life, here's how you do it:

```
for (;;) {
    // Mr. Hammy runs one loop of the
    wheel...Infinitely.
}
```

This will indeed create an infinite loop. Mr. Hammy could be running for all eternity with enough processing power.

However, in Solidity, as we know, computation ain't free. You would use all the gas assigned to that transaction and give it to the miners powering the computation. Expensive. So put parameters in your for loops, let's not kill Mr. Hammy - or let our code run until it chokes on its own gas.

Now let's break down the parts of that complicated looking 'for loop':

- **'For' Keyword**: This tells Solidity that you're about to define, you guessed it, a 'for loop'.

- **Initialisation**: This means 'to start' for those that don't have a well-honed lexical ability in English. This is where you set up the loop in order to keep count of each iteration of it. Is an empty loop
  for (;;) is an empty loop, let's fill it in.

- **Variable Declaration**: For the loop to do anything, you need to create a variable that changes every time the loop completes - no constants here. It's standard practice, or common convention, to simply call this variable 'i'. (i stands for integer). So, the first part of the code now looks like this:
  for (uint i = 0; - now you have a variable, i, that is set to 0.
  Notice how the variable declaration is separated from the next part with a semi colon? That's the syntax of loops (syntax is like grammar for code, remember? It's how it is presented).

- **Condition**: When should the loop stop? This condition will be tested on each run to find out if it is true or false, this determines when the loop stops. In this case, the condition is i < 10, which means the loop continues as long as i is less than 10.
  for (uint i = 0; i < 10; - See? At the start of the first loop, we are at 0. Then, the condition is checked every loop until 'i' reaches the number 10. When it does, the condition that 'i' is smaller than 10 comes out at false, so the loop will not run.

- **The Increment:** This is how we actually increase the value of i every loop. It's the action that gets executed at *the end of each loop iteration*. To do this we use the built in way to increase an integer value by one in solidity which looks like this: '++'.
  When added onto the end of a variable, like i, it increases i by 1. Every time the loop runs, i is increased by 1. **for (uint i = 0; i < 10; i++) {}**
  That's what our loop looks like now. As you might notice, we have an empty code block here, as shown by the empty squiggly brackets {}, so what is that?

- **Loop Body:** This is where you put the code that actually gets executed in each loop iteration. In this case, the loop body is empty, but you could put any code you want in there. It would run a set number of times.

"So when would I use a loop?"

In essence, if you need to perform the same operation multiple times, use a loop. This might be creating a lot of new players for your game, or mapping everyone's addresses to another address, or processing a load of numbers in an array.

You could for example loop over all the integers in the 'potentialDates' array and add them up, then find the mean value of dating potential within the pool.

Loops are a very useful tool in your solidity toolbox.

Escape Artistry: Break & Continue

In Solidity (and most other programming languages), **break** and **continue** are used exclusively within those loops we just learned about.

If loops are one of the tools that let you control the flow of your program, then **break** and **continue** are the tools that let you control the flow within those loops.

Controlflowception: control flow within control flow.

Simply, these two keywords break out of the loop if code finds its mark. For example, if you wanted your loops to end at another condition other than the number of iterations you have set, you could do it like this:

```
for (uint i = 0; i < 10; i++) {
    if (i == 5) {
        break;
    }
    // The loop got to 5! Run Mr. Hammy, save your tiny legs!
}
```

We've seen some of this before.

This declared a 'for loop' that repeated the code in the loop body 10 times. However, in this case, we added a break that stopped the loop if **i** became equal to 5.

Of course, the loop does go to 5, so the loop stopped early, not reaching 10. Let's break down the parts of a break statement in more detail.

You might have noticed we've put an if statement in here, we've seen these before too. It's a way to control structure and flow, I.E the if statement tells Solidity that you're making a decision.

Next, there's the condition. This is trigger for the break. In this case, the condition is **i == 5**, which checks if **i** is equal to 5.

Then, there's the break keyword. This tells Solidity to break out of the loop.

Simple enough.

Now, let's look at a **continue** statement:

```
for (uint i = 0; i < 10; i++) {
    if (i == 5) {
        continue;
    }
    // I am code that runs on every
loop, but if i == 5, it skips the body
of this loop and automatically goes onto
the next iteration!
}
```

It's a little more complex, but not much.

The **continue** statement is used to skip the rest of *the current loop iteration* and immediately start the next iteration. It's often used in conjunction with a conditional statement (**if**) to skip certain iterations of the loop.

To re-iterate. If loops were a casino wheel spin, with the wheel spinning 10 times, the pointer would be landing on numbers from 0 to 9. Every number it lands on is checked, and the function body is executed. Great, the function body contains the code for strippers and free cake.

With **continue**, our wheel (which is, of course, our loop) has a sneaky rule. When the pointer lands on number 5, it's like landing on *skip*.

That's what our if (i == 5) statement is doing - it's checking if we've hit the *skip* segment.

This means that if the pointer lands on 5, no function body is executed - it doesn't end the loop, or stop the game, it just means that for that particular number the code containing strippers and free cake won't run.

Again, the **continue** keyword *skips the rest of the code* immediately but spins the wheel (continues with the next loop iteration) again. No strippers and cake for you, but at least you get to try again!

With **break**, the entire loop is stopped.

This would work better if we randomised the number, of course. It's a pretty game-able casino otherwise, but in essence, that's **break** and **continue**.

Events: The EVM's Facebook Posts

In Solidity, events are used to *log changes* in your code.

They are your speaker system to the entire EVM, blasting out to what's happening inside your contracts. I sometimes use them to say things to Alice. This is how I might define one:

```
event sorryAlice(string message);
```

In this case, the **event** argument is **string** 'message', which means the **event** takes a **string** as an argument and we've called it 'message'.

Now, let's look at how to use it, namely, the **emit** keyword. **Emit** is us grabbing the megaphone and broadcasting an already defined **event** (if you haven't already defined the event and you try to **emit** one, you'll get a 'compilation error' which we are about to go over). So with an **event** & the **emit** keyword, the entire Ethereum 'verse can tune in.

- *event* is how you define.
- *emit* is how you broadcast.
  Like this:

```
Emit messageAlice("Please take me back, Alice, I didn't mean it!");
```

This triggers the MessageAlice event with my heartfelt message. The **emit** keyword must be contained within a function, so all in all it looks like this:

```
pragma solidity ^0.8.0;

contract AliceMessage {

    //let's declare the event name, and the parameters it takes.
    event messageAlice(string message);

    // let's emit the message by calling sendMessage()
    function sendMessage() public {
        emit messageAlice("Please take me back, Alice, I didn't mean it!");
    }
}
```

'This is great', I hear you say, *'I can now broadcast messages.. Somewhere? Now, why on earth would I need to do this? My code should work fine on its own!'*

Well, in Solidity, *everything* is on chain. As solidity is deterministic, getting data *into* your contract from the outside world can be very hard - it requires something called a data oracle. We aren't going to go over these just yet, as we don't yet need to put outside data into our contracts.

But we can get data *out*, for example to a website front end, using logging with event and emit keywords.

Essentially, events provide an easy way for your contract to communicate to the *user facing side* that something happened on the blockchain. This would update the what they actually see on their end, it provides those front-end developers access to all that information via 'listening' for these events. Here's an example of another one in action:

```
pragma solidity ^0.8.0;

contract Events {
    event valueChanged(address indexed author, uint256 oldValue, uint256 newValue);

    uint256 private value;

    function setValue(uint256 newValue) public {
        uint256 oldValue = value;
        value = newValue;
        emit valueChanged(msg.sender, oldValue, newValue);
    }
}
```

Here, we've got an **event** valueChanged. Why is it called that? Because it only gets emitted when the value changes, obviously. Whenever someone, (anyone, as it's public), calls the 'setValue' **function** and sets a new value, this **event** shouts it out to the blockchain. It yells out who did the deed (msg.sender), what the old value was (oldValue), and what the new value is (newValue).

If you were a user of a platform based off of this contract, you wouldn't be watching the blockchain to find out that the value has changed, you wouldn't know how. Therefore, a front end would show you that information via listening out for it and putting into a sexy little user interface – that's what events are for.

'I do think Bitcoin is the first [encrypted money] that has the potential to do something like change the world.'

– **Peter Thiel**

Encountering Wild Errors

In loops, we mentioned that an accidentally coding an infinite loop could result in a 'compile time error'.

This is merely one type of error, and is a small glimpse into what might happen when things go wrong in your contract. Errors will no doubt pop up when you least want them to, at 2am on the last compile of the night, or mid-way through your 187th code wars challenge of the day.

They ruin your flow, and then make you question your life choice on why the fuck you ever decided to sit behind a computer for 12 hours a day frustrated.

Soon you're thinking, *'fuck this, why don't I just go and pour pints?'*.

But fear not, errors are not actually your enemy.

Errors are like that annoying friend who points out every little thing you do wrong. But if you get fat, you better hope there's someone who likes you enough to actually point it out and tells you to stop eating, rather than saying *'Oh... It's been a while. You look, healthy...'*.

It's irritating when people point out that you've put on three stone over lockdown and need to get the fuck out of the house for a run (is that why you left,

Alice?) - but really, they're just trying to help you be better, perhaps get another girlfriend someday.

It's the same with code.

Those errors *will* piss you off, but if you tackle them, soon your DeFi degen coin, NFT shill or J.P Morgan CBDC can buzz along nicely.

So, let's start by understanding what they actually *are*.

What the Hell *is* an Error?

An **error** is Solidity's way of telling you that you fucked it. The system's way of telling you that something in your contract isn't going to go according to plan.

Errors in Solidity come in two flavours:

- **compile-time errors**
- **runtime errors**

Compile-Time Errors

We mentioned these - they're easy to catch, normally easy to fix. These are the mistakes that are caught before you even deploy your contract. They occur when you're trying to actually compile your code (again, bring it from the code you wrote into machine readable gibberish).

Maybe you forgot a semicolon, or you're trying to use a variable that doesn't exist. The compiler catches these errors and gives you a chance to fix them before your code ever sees the depths of the EVM.

Runtime Errors & Exceptions

These lie in wait, hiding in your code until it's executed. As the name suggests, these errors occur when your contract is running, during *run-time*. Maybe you're trying to divide by zero, or a million other ways something can break during runtime. These errors can be harder to catch, but they're just as important to handle.

In Solidity, the terms "exception" and "error" are often used interchangeably - but really, an exception is a type of error. If you want to be a big brained, big dicked Solidity professional, you can specify that exceptions are only encountered *during the execution of a transaction* on the Ethereum network. They are a runtime error.

When they occur occurs, the EVM reverts all changes made by the transaction, ensuring that the blockchain's state remains unchanged. (The gas consumed by the transaction up to the point of the exception is not refunded, it's been spent).

We are just about to look at **Require()** in detail, so don't worry if you don't understand it yet, but the most common exceptions are running out of gas & failing assertions using our three functions. Like:

```
require(someCondition, "You didn't play
by the rules! This is an exception!");
```

In this example, if 'someCondition' is false, the function will throw an exception with the message *"You didn't play by the rules! This is an exception!"*.

Want to make your head hurt? *'All exceptions are runtime errors, but not all runtime errors are exceptions.'* Sounds like some Mensa shit, right. Now you can show off your right sided position on the IQ bell curve at the next programming party you are at, to the one woman that attends.

Dealing with runtime errors means learning how to use those new tools we will soon look at, like **require**, **assert**, and **revert** to further control the flow of your contract and ensure that everything runs smoothly. I'm not going to go into the nitty gritty, exceptions are a type of error - that's all you need to know for now.

Common Errors

Every error is a learning opportunity. Learning what *not* to is just as important as learning what to do. This means learning from others mistakes too (did I mention you should use google a lot?).

These are the usual suspects; you will see lots of these in your development environment of choice.

Syntax Errors, aka Grammar Nazis.

- Miss a semicolon? Syntax error.
- Use an equals sign when you meant to use a double equals sign? Syntax error.
- Forget to close a bracket? You guessed it, syntax error.

These errors are the easiest to fix, you should have a big red error notification at the LoC (line of code) that the error resides in. The compiler will usually tell you where the error is at compile time - easy fix. Even seasoned coders experience this, trust me, don't worry if you get one every time you try to compile.

Type Errors. aka *'what am I?'*

'Maybe I'm a string wrapped in a uint256's body? Maybe I just need therapy?'.

Type errors occur when you try to perform an operation on a variable of the wrong type.

- Trying to add a string to an integer? That's a type error.
- Trying to call a function on a variable that's not a contract? Type error. Again, the compiler will usually tell you what it is and where it is.

Out of Gas Errors aka *'damn, you broke!'*

In Solidity, every operation costs a certain amount of gas. If your contract runs out of gas before it's finished executing, you'll get an out of gas error. This usually means that you're trying to do *too much in a single transaction* (or you've killed Mr.Hammy in an infinite loop). If you're getting out of gas errors, check the loops first, then try and optimise.

Much of the time, it's because the transaction was initiated with an insufficient gas limit, this can happen if the front end of your dApp (decentralised app) is incorrectly estimating gas for your users at the front end - but that's more intermediate stuff.

Revert Errors. aka Takebacksies

Revert errors occur when the **revert()** function is called. This function, as we will further look at, is used to cancel a transaction and refund the remaining gas to the caller. If you're seeing revert errors, it can be a good thing, as something in your contract isn't meeting the conditions set by a **require()** or **assert()** statement, and you are protecting your contract from inputs that don't meet those conditions.

Overflow and Underflow Errors aka *'something doesn't add up..'*

Overflow and underflow errors occur when you try to store a number that's too big or too small for the variable type you're using. For example, if you try to store the number 2^{256} in a **uint256** variable, you'll get an overflow error, because **uint256** variables can only store numbers up to $2^{256} - 1$.

Similarly, if you try to subtract 1 from a **uint256** variable that's currently storing the number 0, you'll get an underflow error, because **uint256** variables can't store negative numbers. We'll look at libraries later that can give you added functionality (and protection) regarding these like *SafeMath*.

Putting Out Fires: Error Handling & Damage Control

Now we know what kind of errors we might face; how do we prepare techniques for when shit does hit the fan?

Compile time errors and bad code that leads to run time errors is all well and good, but what if someone does something to our contract we haven't explicitly coded for?

This might happen by accident or on purpose. This is where three new keywords come in: **revert()**, **require()**, and **assert()**. They are built in functions, so would look like this:

```
revert(condition);
require(condition);
Assert(condition);
```

Revert

The **revert()** function *halts everything,* rolls back any state changes in the current call (the current transaction accessing the function is making this call) and sub-calls (all the calls that have come from this one), and burns the remaining gas.

It stops the transaction in its tracks.

It also lets you throw in a string message to let everyone know *why* the transaction was cancelled, so it can be handy when using DeFi yourself, as it's all on chain. You can go to etherscan (a website that tracks all ether transactions on chain via a website) and find out why your transaction was reverted.

It's also good for you when 'debugging' contracts (finding out what is wrong and fixing it). Let's have a gander at an example of this:

```solidity
pragma solidity ^0.8.0;

contract AhhhImRevertiiinnngggg {
    uint256 public price;

    function setPrice(uint256 _price) public {
        if (_price > 100) {
            revert("Value cannot be more than 100, too expensive!");
        }

// If the input price is over 100, the below line will be skipped completely as the call will be reverted. Therefore the price cannot be set above 100.

        price = _price;
    }
}
```

Further explained, the function setPrice sets the price - but hold on! If you try to set the price to anything more than 100, **revert()** will step in and stop you. It'll burn your gas, halt the transaction and show your error in your transaction - *"Value cannot be more than 100"*.

The price state variable will remain unchanged.

Require

require() is pretty simple too. It requires a condition to execute the code. It's used to validate conditions such as inputs or contract state variables.

It's a bouncer at the door of the function. It checks if the right conditions are met before the party inside can kick off. If they aren't, it reverts the transaction if a condition is not met.

If the conditions inside **require()** come out as false, it'll stop the show, revert all state changes, and *hand back* the remaining gas to the caller.

Let's see **require()** in action:

```
pragma solidity ^0.8.0;

contract PartyTime {
    uint256 public instagramFollowers;

    function enterClub(uint256 _instagramFollowers) public {
        require(_instagramFollowers >= 1000, "You need more followers to party here, we are vapid and shallow people");
        instagramFollowers = _instagramFollowers; //This won't run if
```

```
    the number of followers is lower than
    1000
        }
}
```

In the 'enterClub' **function**, **require()** is the bouncer checking the _instagramFollowers at the door. If the _instagramFollowers are less than 1000, **require()** will shut the door, throwing the *"You need more followers to party here, we are vapid and shallow people"* out as a reason.

Any gas that was set aside for the function will be returned, sans a little taken for the computational trouble.

Assert()

This function catches those bugs that shouldn't happen at all.

assert() should be used for conditions that *must never be false* and would indicate a serious error in the code. For checks that validate user input or external factors, it's typically more appropriate to use **require()**, which also reverts the transaction if the condition is false, but does not consume all remaining gas.

Although they seem similar, **require()** is used to validate the inputs and ensure that the conditions for a valid transfer are met, while **assert()** is used to check an invariant that *must always hold true*, and its failure would indicate a serious bug in the contract.

If **assert()** comes across a condition that gives a big fat false, it slams the brakes on the transaction and takes all the remaining gas.

Unlike its siblings **require()** and **revert()**, it doesn't take an optional error message. It just ends things, plain and simple. Check out assert() in action:

```
pragma solidity ^0.8.0;

contract CheckImportantStuff {
    function calculate(uint256 a, uint256 b) public pure returns (uint256)
{
        uint256 result = a + b;
        assert(result >= a);
// This is double-checking we haven't bumped into an overflow
        return result;
    }
}
```

In the CheckImportantStuff function, assert() is watching. Alwaaays watchinggg.

It's making sure the sum of a and b hasn't resulted in an integer overflow, a common mishap in the coding world before SafeMath. We've come across this SafeMath calculation before, this just has a little more added. Here, if **assert()** sees something wrong—like the sum being smaller than one of the added numbers (which would mean an overflow happened)—it'll halt everything and take all the remaining gas with it.

It's assert's job to catch the coding bugs that are a huge no-no, perhaps regarding incorrect calculation of funds, or potential security issues.

In older versions of Solidity (before 0.5.0), **throw** was used to handle error conditions and exceptions. When executed, it reverted all changes made to the state during the current call (and all its sub-calls) and depleted all remaining gas. Like this:

```
if (condition: shit hits the fan) {
    throw;}
```

When you read this book, we are already past solidity version v0.8.21, so it's been a while. Even though throw isn't used in new Solidity contracts, it's important to understand it if you're looking at older contracts or legacy code.

'Internet 'may just be a passing fad' as millions give up on it'

- Daily Mail, Tuesday, December 5th, 2000.

The Perfect Contract Blueprint

I am once again asking for you to declare a contract.

Get it? That Bernie Sanders thing? When you spent your entire life online, you begin to only speak in memes.

Jokes are way funnier when you have to explain them, too.

Anyway, we're going back to the basics

```
contract Example {
    /* As we know, all of your shitty junior solidity dev code goes here, this is where you really earn that 250k a year. */
}
```

Time to learn more about contract anatomy. This is more of a 'best practice', as if you declare a state variable, it can go anywhere, really. However, keeping code organised, even when you're writing small contracts, is important - both for reading the code of others and having others read your code. Not to mention reading back your code yourself.

Contracts usually share a certain structure:

```
//version control:
pragma solidity ^0.8.0;
```

```solidity
//Declare the contract name:
contract PokemonCreator {

//The contract will usually start by declaring all the state variables for use within the contract:
    uint public pokemonCount;
    address public owner;

//Then the 'events' will be defined:
    event NewPokemon(uint pokemonCount);

//Next, modifiers used within the contract (libraries are coming up soon, which can contain all these, so you may skip this part in simple code):
    modifier onlyOwner() {
        require(msg.sender == owner);
        _;
    }

//Next, lots of contracts will set themselves as the 'owner' of the contract on deployment:
    constructor() public {
        owner = msg.sender;   // Set contract deployer as owner
    }

//Only now does the meat of the contract come in, the functions:
    function createPokemon() public onlyOwner {
        pokemonCount++;
        emit NewPokemon(pokemonCount);
    }
}
```

A quick explanation of what is happening here, and why:

First off, we've got our *state variables*. They come first so you can easily keep track of them. Here we have 'pokemonCount' as the headcount of our pokemon, and 'owner' is the lucky trainer who gets to call themselves the Pokemaster.

Next up, we've got our **event**, 'NewPokemon'. We learned how these work earlier and how to **emit** them.

Then we've got the modifier **onlyOwner**. This only lets the 'owner' address use this function, if anyone else tries they will receive an error. We defined the owner in the **constructor** function. This is set on deployment, as we've looked at.

Finally, we've got our functions, in our case, the 'createPokemon' function. Only the owner can create more little poke-mans (I like saying it like this, it's funnier). When they do, the 'pokemonCount' increases by one, and the 'NewPokemon' event gets triggered, letting everyone know there's a new Pokemon in the grass to catch.

So, there you have it, contract anatomy.

Inheritance: Virtual Daddy Issues

Can't be bothered to write you own code?

Me neither.

For our penultimate chapter, we're going to look at inheritance, which is a way to *share code* across contracts. It allows contracts to inherit variables and functions from other contracts on the EVM (or locally at compile time).

This is done using the **is** keyword. Let's break this down.

Firstly, it looks like this:

```
contract Prince is King {
 // Normal contract code here
}
```

The contract you are working with here is called Prince - that's how you've defined it.

But Prince is also 'King' - meaning you have inherited all the contract code from another contract called 'King'. (Except private variables and functions). A contract that is being inherited *from* is called a **parent contract** or base contract, and the contract that inherits it is called a **child contract** or derived contract.

Think of it like a Royal Family, the king (parent contract) has all the power (functions) and wealth (state variables), and the prince (child contract) inherits all of it, except for the king's secret stash (private variables and functions).

Basically, the derived contract inherits all non-private state variables and functions from the base contract. Here's a simple example:

```
contract King {
    function execute() public pure returns (string memory) {
        return "Off with his head, I'm fucking royalty!";
    }
}


contract Prince is King {
    // Prince can now use execute()
}
```

The **Prince** contract is the heir to the **King** contract. This means that **Prince** can now use the execute() function just like the **King**! Pretty cool, apart from the fact that he's 7 years old - and very spoiled - so you better give him a wide berth.

Virtual and override keywords

Let's say you want to create a function in your contract. Fine, we know how to do that:

```
function doSomething() public returns (string memory) {
```

```
    return "I returned a string that is
not in storage";
}
```

Okay, so what if you've inherited from another contract that has a function of the same name?

You will need the **override** keyword.

```
function doSomething() public override
returns (string memory) {
    return "I returned a string that
wasn't in storage";
}
```

That would allow you to declare a function that takes precedent over the other function, overriding it.

However - you may get an error as in order to *be able* to **override** this function name that's been inherited, the functions from the inherited contract must be specified as **virtual**. This means the original function would actually have to include one more keyword, **virtual**. This would look like this:

function doSomething() public virtual returns (string memory) {
    return "I returned a string that is not in storage";
}

Libraries: Borrowing Brilliance

Libraries make life a lot easier. Which is fitting for our final chapter in the *Basics* book.

As a dev, you are going to want to do as little mundane work as possible. This means for example, that for every contract you write, you really don't want to be writing out a whole bunch of really common modifiers that you use all the time.

This is where libraries come in.

Libraries in Solidity are similar to regular contracts, with some key differences (and restrictions), overall, they're great for creating *reusable code* and complex data structures.

They may not have their own storage or hold Ether, but they're packed with tools that can be used in other contracts.

They're a bit like how you would reference data from a real-life library - and yes - I hear you;

'I'm no boomer, I've never seen the inside of this 'library', I use GOOGLE, what's the purpose of one?'

I hear you, my zoomie-zoom friend, thanks for putting down Tik-Tok for long enough to learn something useful.

The primary purpose of libraries is to provide a way to share common utility functions or algorithms across multiple contracts - by using libraries, you avoid repeating the same code in multiple places, leading to more efficient and maintainable contracts.

If you have a bunch of contracts that are all going to be using the same specific functions, chuck them all into a library and refer to it in your code. It's a bit like **inheritance** except libraries aren't deployed on chain like other contracts, they're linked on contract compilation at the bytecode level.

Put simply, this means all the stuff the library does is already in your contract as soon as it's deployed - the trade-off is that you can't simply 'update' the library that you contract is linked to. If you need a function within that library to change, you're gonna need to compile yourself a whole new contract.

A Library All of Your Own

Let's be frank, you aren't going to be defining your own libraries in your first contracts, you will only begin to reference from others.

Let's just look at how you would do it, so you can get your head around the syntax, though. It's just like declaring a contract, except you'd use the **library** keyword:

```
library SafeMath {
    function add(uint256 a, uint256 b)
internal pure returns (uint256) {
        uint256 c = a + b;
        require(c >= a, "SafeMath: addition overflow");
        return c;
    }
}
```

This is a snippet of the SafeMath library, can you see what it might do? Have a look and take a guess.

(Yes, we've seen this).

Okay ready?

Well, as we mentioned in 'data types', integers in solidity can sometimes overflow. This means that over a certain number, they will loop back around to 0.

This could be a huge problem in DeFi, as if a contract's integers do not add up correctly someone may end up getting more or less funds than they should.

This function simply checks that adding two numbers together does not return a smaller number. Remember. You can refer back to **operators** if you are unsure what some of these are.

Restrictions on Libraries

There are quite a few restrictions with Libraries, a lot stemming from the fact that they don't actually exist on chain at a fixed address, except in your already deployed contracts bytecode. Libraries therefore:

- Cannot store state variables, as *they don't have internal storage*. This restriction exists to ensure that libraries are 'stateless' and only contain reusable logic.

- Cannot inherit from or be inherited by other contracts.

- Cannot receive ether in transactions. (Where would you send it?).

Function Modifiers in Libraries:

Libraries can still use function modifiers, so you can set pre- or post-conditions to multiple functions in the library, for example some libraries might have the **onlyOwner** modifier on some functions.

Internal Visibility:

All functions inside a library are implicitly defined as **internal**.

In practice, this means they can only be accessed by the contract that calls the library. These functions are not visible to other contracts in the system.

Using Custom libraries yourself:

To use a library, you have to *import it* into your contract.

If you wanted to use a specific library you defined in a local file (let's say you called it 'ThisIsALibrary.sol'), then you would have to use some code to make sure it is imported at compile time.

This would mean you'd be working with two files. One, of course, would be your contract, let's just call it 'MyContract.sol' and the other would be your custom library, 'ThisIsALibrary.sol'.

To do this you'd use an **import** statement:

```
import "./ThisIsALibrary.sol";
```

After importing, you can access the functions of the library directly without the need to copy all of the library's code to your code - technically it has already been copied in - with just that one **import** statement

This is easy enough, but where does it go? It goes *above* where you define your contract, not inside it. It's outside the contract's scope, as the contract has to inherit from it. Like this:

```solidity
// SPDX-License-Identifier: MIT
pragma solidity ^0.8.0;

import "./ThisIsALibrary.sol";

contract MyContract {
//Code here
}
```

And Wahlah! You now have access to everything that you or someone else defined in the library! Let's look at how you might actually *use* the functions of a library. Here's an example:

```solidity
import "./ThisIsALibrary.sol";

contract ContractUsingLibraries {

    function aContractFunction() public
{
        uint256 result =
ThisIsALibrary.aLibraryFunction();
    }
}
```

Okay so this might need some explaining.

In order to access aLibraryFunction() within ./ThisIsALibrary.sol we are first defining a function within our own contract called aContractFunction(), then *within this*, we have this line of code:

```solidity
uint256 result =
ThisIsALibrary.aLibraryFunction();
```

Let's start with the easy bit.

First, we defined result as a **uint256**.

Then, we used the = operator to make 'result' the product of calling the aLibraryFunction() *within* ThisIsALibrary.

To do this, we used dot notation to specify that, first, the library name was ThisIsALibrary. Then we used a dot (.), to specify that *within* that library the function we needed was aLibraryFunction().

If this takes a while to sink in, don't worry. At the start of your contract writing, you will mostly be using *standard libraries*.

Standard Libraries

As we know, unlike regular contracts, libraries are not deployed independently.

Instead, they are linked to the contract that uses them at compile time, this is automatic if you use the **import** keyword. When you compile a contract that uses a library, the compiler effectively incorporates all the library's functions into the contract.

Solidity provides some **standard libraries**, such as *SafeMath* (are you getting sick of *SafeMath* as an example yet? You shouldn't be, I bet you'll use it) which contains arithmetic functions with overflow and underflow checks to help prevent common vulnerabilities in smart contracts.

(I know you know this, but hacks for hundreds of millions have occurred because someone missed the **import** line and didn't use underflow or overflow checks.)

The SafeMath library is part of the OpenZeppelin library (openzeppelin-contracts), which is a popular set of reusable smart contracts developed and audited by the OpenZeppelin team.

They know their stuff, and have many libraries you can import from. You'd import it like this:

```
import "@openzeppelin/contracts/utils/math/SafeMath.sol";
```

The "@" symbol in the import statement is new for us here.

It's used to specify a 'path' to the library. These @ paths are not just used for libraries, they can be used to locate external contracts and interfaces that your contract might depend on.

When you use an **import** statement, the compiler needs to know the exact path to find the referenced file - so using an 'alias' with the "@" symbol allows you to define a shorter, more readable name for a long path.

It makes your import statements cleaner and easier to manage, especially when dealing with long and nested directory structures.

Once imported, a library like SafeMath can be specified a bit differently. You can implement its functions for all uints with this piece of code:

```
using SafeMath for uint;
```

All in all, it looks like this:

```
import "@openzeppelin/contracts/utils/math/SafeMath.sol";
```

```
contract MathStuff {
    using SafeMath for uint;

    function add(uint a, uint b) public
pure returns (uint) {
        return a.add(b);
    }}
```

Alright, this is pretty intense for a new solidity learner, almost there.

This means that the contract is now using all of the functions defined for the data type 'uint' throughout the contract. Now uints cannot overflow.

This is a simple way of making your contracts more robust and a way to have more complex mechanisms supporting them, all with a simple import statement.

These OpenZeppelin libraries are written by the best, and they're freely accessible for everyone, they're certainly worth using instead of making your own custom contracts.

Anyway, there's another benefit to libraries - deployment cost savings. In essence, libraries can save gas.

This is more advanced stuff, that delves into bytecode duplication, but you don't really need to worry about until you've deployed a fair few contracts, so I won't iterate more. (let's just manage to deploy one shite contract before we worry about the minutia of gas cost savings).

Okay, libraries are done, but make sure to look over this again when you are actually writing a contract to see how this works again.

Let us conclude.

'Bitcoin was created to serve a highly political intent, a free and uncensored network where all can participate with equal access.'

– Amir Taaki

The End of the Basics: Preparing for Intermediate Solidity

We made it. This book has covered the basics of solidity, for consumption in book form.

It's a tool. One of many in your programming toolbox, and although it's only an overview of how solidity works, I hope it's one you can come back to often while you are learning.

I have included a list of further resources at the bottom of the page for you to take a look at when you are at a computer – but if you aren't, and won't be for a while, the next book in this series, *Intermediate Solidity for Degens*, may be out – there's no time like the present to continue the process while it's still fresh.

For now, I'll say that we've come a hell of a long way, but here's a tip from someone who has been around the block both in life and in programming:

Repetition works.

Although it does sound kind of lame, it doesn't have to be. It's a fundamental aspect of learning, and it has been studied extensively in cognitive psychology and educational research.

My point? This book is not designed to be read once; it's designed to be a guide you can refer back to for the basics of solidity.

It's designed to shock you into remembering some otherwise pretty dense stuff!

Structs are pretty boring, okay, I admit it. But make them a 'SexDrawer'? That's weird enough that you just might remember you put things inside of it.

I'm talking about the drawer. Putting things inside *the drawer*. I'm not talking about putting things inside anywhere else...

This way of learning tickles your brain in such a way that makes long-term retention of information easier.

Space out the revisits, too. Keep the book handy, and instead of scrolling mindlessly through the newest brain destroying app, pick this up instead and review data types. You don't have to spend hours doing it, just to it for 10 minutes.

The point I'm trying to get across - read this over again - you've earned a rest now, lord knows. But maybe tomorrow, or the next day.

Read this again.

If I finish a book, I rarely read it just once. Here's my reasoning:

If I've got to the end of it, it held my attention for long enough to be worthwhile. If it did that, it had some good takeaways I'd like to implement in my skillset or mindset. If it did that, I'm going to want to make sure I remember them, so I'll make sure I read it often.

If you do go onto the next book. It will of course recap *some* of the basics, but you'll need much of the knowledge from this book to get anywhere with the next one.

So, before moving onto intermediate, I'd suggest completely mastering the concepts explained within this book.

If you are finished for now though, celebrate a little! You know what smart contracts are, what they contain, and how the features within them work. *Most of the world will never know as much as you know now.* They won't know it when they take out that smart contract travel insurance, or when they pay via smart contract, or even *get married* on chain. You know how it works though, well done.

I truly believe that the more programmers learn solidity as a language, the better our society will become, as more and more centralised power will be distributed to the people. You are now part of that, and you should be proud.

Next Steps

Call me old fashioned, but sometimes I just need a book. That's why I wanted to make this guide in the first place. Everything is so *online* these days. What if I'm on a plane without Wi-Fi? Or I want to give my eyes a break from incessant blue glare?

That said, online is where you will find some fantastic resources regarding solidity. Now you have a grasp of the basics, I'd recommend some websites where you can put your skills to the test, and reinforce your knowledge. I recommend these free resources in ascending order of difficulty.

CryptoZombies.io

CryptoZombies is an interactive online platform that offers a unique and engaging way to learn Solidity programming. Here's what makes it special:

- Interactive Coding Lessons: CryptoZombies provides in-browser step-by-step lessons that guide you from the very basics of Solidity to creating your own fully-functional blockchain-based game.
- Build a Zombie Army: The platform allows you to build a zombie army (with NFTs) It's half code-school, half MMO crypto-collectible strategy game.

Solidity by Example.org

Solidity by Example is a practical website that offers hands-on examples of Solidity code. Although a bit dense, it can be good to reference.

- Practical Examples: The site provides real-world examples of Solidity code, covering various topics like primitives, structures, error handling, and more.
- Suitable for Beginners: The examples are explained in a simple and understandable manner, making it

suitable for those new to Solidity.

Ethernaut by OpenZeppelin

Ethernaut is a Web3/Solidity based wargame developed by OpenZeppelin. It's a bit more intermediate, but here's what you can expect:

- Challenging Puzzles: Ethernaut presents Solidity and Ethereum smart contract security challenges that users must solve by hacking the contracts.
- Learn by Doing: The platform encourages hands-on learning, where users learn about security best practices by actively exploiting vulnerabilities.
- Community Support: Ethernaut has a strong community of developers and enthusiasts who can provide support and guidance through the challenges.

So, these courses and tutorials offer extra ways to improve your solidity skills with a couple of different approaches.

As well as these, I would also recommend the fantastic YouTube videos by Patrick Collins using a variety of different frameworks to learn solidity. (Frameworks are in the next book).

Whether you prefer interactive gaming experiences, hands-on coding examples, academic courses, or security challenges, there's something for every aspiring Solidity developer out there,

Check them out if you can, if not, I'll see you in the next one. Keep calm, and carry on coding.

"The technology of the Information Age makes it possible to create assets that are outside the reach of many forms of coercion.

This new asymmetry between protection and extortion rests upon a fundamental truth of mathematics."

– James Dale Davidson

ABOUT THE AUTHOR

C.J Freeman is an avid programmer turned early-stage investor/advisor. He specialises in web 3.0 companies and platforms focusing on blockchain technology (Bitcoin, Ethereum, Chainlink, Pocket Network).

When occasionally on social media, he tweets from the moniker @tripsdiamond, at least until a decentralised alternative comes around. He is a staunch advocate of free speech and decentralising legacy finance, and hates talking about himself in third person.

COPYRIGHT

ISBN: 9798858885047 (paperback)
ASIN: B0CGKDJB5G (eBook)

This edition published in 2023
Copyright © C.J Freeman 2023
Published by Aquila Press Ltd

C.J Freeman has asserted his right to be identified as the author of this work in accordance with the Copyright, Designs and Patents Act 1988.

All rights reserved. No part of this publication may be reproduced, stored in a retrieval system, or transmitted in any form or by any means, electronic, mechanical, photocopying, recording or otherwise, without the prior permission of the copyright owner. Any unauthorised distribution or use of this text may be a direct infringement of the author's and publisher's rights and those responsible may be liable in law accordingly.

Printed in Great Britain
by Amazon